All Mains
Cultus Lake
B.C.

PAPER WHEAT

Created by 25th Street Theatre

PAPER WHEAT
THE BOOK

Western Producer Prairie Books
Saskatoon, Canada

Publication of this book has been assisted by
The Canada Council and the Saskatchewan
Arts Board.

Jacket and book design by Steve Tate, GDL.

Printed and bound in Canada by
Modern Press
Saskatoon, Saskatchewan

Western Producer Prairie Book publications are
produced and manufactured in the middle of
Western Canada by a unique publishing
venture owned by a group of prairie farmers
who are members of Saskatchewan Wheat
Pool. From the first book published in 1954, a
reprint of a serial originally carried in the
weekly newspaper, *The Western Producer,* to
the book before you now, the tradition of
providing enjoyable and informative reading
for all Canadians is continued.

Canadian Cataloguing in Publication Data

Twenty-fifth Street House Theatre.
    Paper wheat

    ISBN 0-88833-079-0

    1. Twenty-fifth Street House Theatre. Paper
wheat. I. Title.
PS8589.W46P3   C812'.54   C82-091014-7
PR9199.3.T93P3

Dedicated to the Board of Directors of 25th Street Theatre who have enthusiastically supported this important and aggressive professional theatre throughout the years: Ben Mckinnon, E. C. Partridge, Gary Rathgeber, Lynden Hillier, Holly Ann Knott, Betty Ann Heggie, Richard Roberts, Gerry Stoll, Ollie Cowan, Joan Frederickson, Stuart Poole and Dr. Zenon Belak.

Contents

Acknowledgments

25th Street Theatre gratefully acknowledges the assistance of:

The Touring Office of the Canada Council
The Saskatchewan Arts Board
The City of Saskatoon
Sask Sport Trust
Saskatchewan Wheat Pool
Alberta Wheat Pool
Department of Cooperatives, Province of Saskatchewan

All production photographs (unless otherwise indicated) courtesy of Patrick Close

Historical photographs courtesy of Saskatchewan Archives

A Short History of the Co-operative Movement in Saskatchewan

A Short History of the Co-operative Movement in Saskatchewan

John Archer

"God had sifted three kingdoms to find wheat for this planting."
—Longfellow

The settlement of Canada's agricultural West was a long time coming. There had been fully a quarter century of hopes deferred. But during the decade and a half prior to World War I, the long-awaited rush of homesteaders materialized. Millions of immigrants from eastern Canada, the United States, the United Kingdom, and continental Europe poured into the West in a mass migration that attracted worldwide interest and that appeared to feed and flourish on its own success. In the euphoria of the moment, Prime Minister Wilfrid Laurier could publicly declare that the twentieth century belonged to Canada.

The people responsible for this triumph were the homesteaders, those unsung thousands who settled the frontier. Early on, the Dominion government had set up immigration offices in the United States, the United Kingdom, and in key locations in continental Europe. Together with the Canadian Pacific Railway, the government sent out information and propaganda designed to attract immigrants with the offer of cheap passage and free land. The immigration sheds in Canada received these would-be pioneers as they landed, processed them, and directed them to waiting trains, which in turn trundled them across forest land, Shield country, and miles of wilderness to Winnipeg, the gateway to the West. There officials sorted the newcomers by regional destination and directed them to land offices in Yorkton, Saskatoon, Battleford, Swift Current, Moose Jaw, Regina. This meant another train journey in the meager comfort of the colonist cars. There was then a long wait in lineups outside the land office before one could file on a

homestead. Then came that last trek by wagon to the chosen quarter section, 160 acres of virgin prairie that was to be home. A long, wearing journey, with spirits roiled by hopes, expectations, fears, challenges. Thus Sean, Vasil, Anna, Elizabeth, and William — Irish, Ukrainian, Latvian, and English — enter the story, on a train heading west to Saskatchewan.

They came to a seemingly empty land, an expanse of wilderness that stretched beyond imagination. It had been the haunt of the Indian, the territory of the fur trader, the native ground of the Métis. After 1870, as the Canadian North-West, it had frustrated the dreams and plans of a Canadian government hoping to emulate the success of the Americans in subdividing their West. Yet the blueprint of a future was there, in place: a form of government to administer this, the North-West Territories; a mounted police force to keep the Queen's peace. The land had been surveyed, and a homestead law enacted. The Indians had been persuaded to move onto reserves. In due course, the Canadian Pacific Railway was completed across the prairies and through the mountains to the far western ocean. Surely this fulfillment of a most ambitious undertaking would be the key to rapid settlement. And yet the land lay empty. The Métis under Louis Riel and his able lieutenant, Gabriel Dumont, were pushed aside. The National Policy was set in place, a concept that would see a web of tariffs, finance, commerce, and transportation bind the far-flung elements of a country together. And still the land lay empty, save for a handful of settlers from Ontario and those few colonists from the United Kingdom and Europe that had been brought in under various schemes.

But everything came right as the century turned, and it was conditions outside of Canada

3

that made the difference. Money became more plentiful as the long depression of the late nineteenth century lessened and prices rose. Markets for foodstuffs expanded as western Europe became industrialized. Transatlantic cargo rates for grain were lowered. A reduction of international tensions in Europe permitted more liberal emigration policies on that continent. And most significantly perhaps, the price of land in the American Midwest increased as that frontier filled up. The farmlands of western Canada became attractive as never before. Canadian authorities took advantage of the new opportunities, and a polygot stream of humanity poured into the "last best West" on the Canadian prairies.

There were those among the newcomers who would speculate in land, but these were a minority. The vast majority sought a homestead and a new start in life. American settlers brought with them experience in dry-land farming and the capital and equipment to make a successful start. Ukrainians, Germans, Hungarians, and others from the Baltic, lower Danube, and the steppes brought experience in farming and a sense of community and identity. Scandinavians were familiar with the practices of democracy and were, for the most part, farmers and woodsmen. Many of the immigrants from the United Kingdom were city born, moving from one patch of red on the map to another, and were surprised to find new and unexpected challenges. They knew the language and customs and were able to use these advantages to establish themselves in occupations other than farming. The Canadians who came from "down east" were themselves of pioneer stock and were at home on a developing frontier.

This influx of settlers set the machinery of Canada's National Policy into humming high gear. The grand design called for an industrial center in Ontario and Quebec that drew much of its economic lifeblood from the exploitation of the vast agricultural hinterland. Thus, factories in central Canada expanded and worked longer hours to meet the demand for consumer goods, machinery, and equipment. Financial houses engaged western managers trained to distinguish assets from optimism. The railways — the Canadian Pacific and its later rivals — ran loaded west and east as an outgoing torrent of golden wheat met the mixed trainloads of incoming colonists and goods. There was ever a cry for more railways, more trains, more boxcars.

An adequate system of transportation was one of the prime requisites for success in settling the prairie West. Only a railway could provide a relatively cheap and rapid means of transporting bulk products, such as wheat, to ports for export, and people and goods from ports and inland cities to the western stations. No rapid settlement of the Canadian West was possible without the railway. No remote areas could be settled and become productive without expansion of the system to serve such areas. Settlers appreciated the importance of the railroad. Proximity to such a facility enhanced the value of farm lands. On the other hand, settlers soon learned that the railroad officials obeyed dictates from head offices back east and paid little heed to the particular likes or needs of the individual farmer. Certainly farmers appeared to have little influence on rates or timetables. Very early western settlers developed a love-hate relationship with the Canadian Pacific.

A similar ambiguity existed in the home-steaders' feelings about their land. Theirs was no easy life: there were few amenities, fewer guarantees. People from all over the world had been scattered broadcast over the lonely reaches of the West. Few had much in the way of financial resources; each had an all-consuming desire to own land. Every family faced the same basic challenges imposed by distance and climate. For the women, in particular, isolation was an insidious foe. The man of the family could see his neighbors at work or in town. The pioneer wife was less fortunate, shut in over a long winter with no female companionship. Summers were little better if her man had to find work in some distant area in order to earn cash to buy winter provisions. Then the woman must assume full responsibility for home, children, livestock. Fires and blizzards could kill. Hail and drought or grasshoppers could destroy the crop. Isolation and loneliness could destroy the spirit. For men and women alike, the accent was on strength, hardihood, adaptability. There was an awareness of basic needs and an emphasis, in the early years, on survival and security.

But homestead life was not all hardship and forebearance. With Anna, in Swift Current, one senses the excitement of building. The sights, sounds, and smells of a community in the making speak powerfully of the dynamic energy of the frontier. We share with Anna the delight in finding something familiar, something of home in this alien world. It seems but right and fitting that Anna and Vasil should come to an understanding, break with the proprieties of the time, and marry forthwith. One might be lonely on the frontier, but one did not live alone. Neighbors were important. They were needed, in good times and in bad. Thus Vasil offers William his plow when he sees that

his neighbor's plow is broken. William helps dig a well for Vasil in return. Immediate need overcame the wall of strangeness. For the most practical of reasons, cooperation early became a convention of prairie life.

The odds against instant success on the western frontier were prohibitive, though the chances of ultimate victory were somewhat better. Many homesteaders fell victims to inexperience, drought, debt, or accident. Certainly natural causes brought about many trials and hardships. But these were not the only obstacles. There were others devised by men, both in distant places and close at hand. Thus John, the storekeeper, takes advantage of his customers by extending credit on terms that ensure return of his goods if not paid for out of the next year's crop. He sells Vasil horses, equipment, and food — much of which is going out "for the fifth time." Such happenings were common. But the more lasting hurts were inflicted by organized commercial and financial interests determined to exploit the opportunity for gain that was presented by the western boom. To the farmer, the entrenched interests of the railway, the line elevator companies, the Winnipeg Grain Exchange, and the banks were the real enemy. They were not across the counter, within arm's reach, where one could "get some exercise" but were distant, impersonal, implacable enemies.

Almost from the beginning, there had been a tradition of political protest in the Canadian West. The settlers who came in before 1896, few though they were, left their mark in politics, education, and government. They understood the parliamentary process and were accustomed to political expression. Very early, they devised vehicles for organized dissent, in order to have their voices heard in the House of Commons. The immigrants who came so hopefully at the

5

turn of the century built on the experience of the earlier homesteaders and used channels of communication and protest already open. Thus it was that farm leaders looked to their elected representatives for redress of their grievances and importuned governments to control freight rates, to standardize grading and weighing practices in the grain trade, and to set prices for grain. In those early days there was little thought that farmers or government might play an active role in selling grain internationally.

Numbers weighed in the farmers' favor as united, they gained the Crow's Nest Rates on grain in 1897. In 1900 Parliament passed the Manitoba Grain Act which set out rules and regulations governing the handling, grading, and shipment of grain. The value of such statutory enactments was made clear when farmers took the Canadian Pacific Railway to court for failure to observe the provisions of the law. This, the famous Sintaluta case, restored the right of farmers to obtain cars for loading in strict rotation of application. Pressure from farmers led to the appointment of a royal commission to study and report on the grain trade. Disappointed that the report of this body did not recommend public ownership of terminal elevators and legislation to regulate the mixing of grades, a delegation of farmers went to Ottawa to present a "farmers' platform" to members of the House of Commons. Such action drew public attention to the farmers' complaints.

Effective pressure on governments depended to a large extent on effective organization at the farm level. Farm leaders needed organized support if they were to impress distant politicians. There had been early attempts to form farmers' unions in Manitoba and the North-West Territories, but each had met with only passing success. In 1901 a situation occurred which so enraged farmers that they flung themselves into an organized and lasting association. That year, there was a bumper crop; there was also a shortage of grain cars. As a consequence, country elevators were congested to the point that frustrated farmers described conditions as a "wheat blockade." Elevator agents took advantage of these events by refusing to accept grain at top grades but offering to take it in at a lower grade. The farmer had the option of accepting a grade which he knew to be lower than he deserved or of taking the grain home. This was no choice at all as Vasil and William and Sean knew, for they had to sell grain in order to pay for equipment they had bought or see that equipment revert to John, the slick storekeeper. Small wonder that the trio agreed to visit the local elevator agent for a little "exercise."

But while "exercise" might temporarily relieve frustrations, it would not make for a lasting cure. Other action might. John A. Miller of Indian Head called a protest meeting of farmers late in 1901, and out of that meeting there came the decision to form a permanent association. Thus the Territorial Grain Growers' Association came into being in 1902. The presidency went to a well-known local farmer, W. R. Motherwell. When the province of Saskatchewan was created in 1905, the organization was renamed the Saskatchewan Grain Growers' Association.

One of the pioneer members of the SGGA, Ed A. Partridge, hoped to persuade the association to undertake cooperative handling and marketing of grain. The leadership was cautious, loath to enter this new field and thus to challenge the mighty. Partridge was supported by a number of farmers, however, and the group formed the Grain Growers' Grain Company, with Partridge as president. The company bought a seat on the Winnipeg Grain Exchange and began handling grain. Their avowed policy was to pay patronage dividends to supporters in accordance with cooperative principles. The Exchange immediately reacted by refusing to permit the company to market grain through Exchange facilities. The Manitoba government intervened, and the GGG Company was reinstated, but only on condition that it forego the payment of patronage dividends. There were further attempts to kill the upstart company but, with the resignation of Partridge as president and the election of T. A. Crerar, an uneasy working relationship developed and the farmers' company became a recognized force in the grain-marketing world.

Meanwhile, Partridge, who by this time had moved to Winnipeg, had become impressed by the power and influence of the newspaper press in that city. He persuaded the GGG Company to establish a newspaper of its own — an organ that would explain to farmers how grain was gathered, sold, and delivered and that would present a rural point of view on national problems. The *Grain Growers' Guide* began publication in 1908 with Partridge as editor. He gave up this responsibility almost at once but continued to work for the farm movement's objectives. In 1925, he set out his philosophy in a book entitled *A War on Poverty*, in which he outlined the ideal of a cooperative commonwealth, a world based on cooperative enterprise.

Farm leaders had long pressed for Dominion ownership of the terminals and territorial (or provincial) control of the inland elevators. Farmer conventions annually approved these broad objectives. With the creation of two new provinces, Alberta and Saskatchewan, in 1905, the focus of the campaign was shifted to prairie governments, and local politicians were forced to meet the challenge. In 1911, Premier Scott of Saskatchewan adroitly fended off the pressure for government ownership in his province by bringing forward legislation incorporating the Saskatchewan Co-operative Elevator Company. This cooperative enterprise was farmer-owned and farmer-controlled. Backed by government loans, it was a successful undertaking, with Charles Dunning (a man who was to make his mark in various fields of endeavour) as the first secretary-treasurer. Farmers could now control a portion more of their economic destiny.

During this period, there were leaders among the women of the frontier as well. Lillian Beynon, Cora Hind, Nellie McClung, Violet McNaughton, and others organized Homemakers' Clubs, called for libraries, and found ways and means to pass along information on homemaking, gardening, and organizing. Much attention was focused on the establishment of churches, the attainment of prohibition, and the provision of health services. But there was self-interest as well as selfless devotion in the women's campaigns. Generally, husband and wife were partners in the pioneering enterprise. Yet there was, under the existing laws, the possibility that a husband might sell the family farm, quite legally, without the wife's consent. Indeed, he might desert his wife and children. Women worked for, and won, changes in the Homestead Act to correct this situation. But there were other injustices calling for correction, and the corrective process was slow. The women realized, as had their male counterparts, that the springs of power lay in government. A strong movement for female suffrage developed, and in 1916 Saskatchewan women gained the right to vote in provincial elections. Again, it was the power of organized numbers that won the day.

The Great War, 1914-18, brought an end to the period of rapid immigration. It cast a pall over the settlement process in Saskatchewan, as thousands of homesteaders joined up to fight overseas, and it caused a serious dislocation of the grain trade. While the call to fight for one's country cooled the heat of farm protests, the fires were but banked and would flare up when stirred anew. The Dominion government assumed wide powers of control over the grain trade since foodstuffs were considered to be munitions of war. The Crow rates were suspended. The Winnipeg Grain Exchange was closed. A Canadian Wheat Board was set up to sell the 1918 crop. The formation of a Union government disrupted old party loyalties.

War's end brought a renewal of farmer unrest. The government abolished the Wheat Board, though it had been popular with farmers. The Winnipeg Grain Exchange was permitted to reopen, but the Crow rates were not restored. Then came the spark that reignited the farmers' protest — a drastic drop in prices. Farmers, through their various associations, had generally supported lower tariffs, abolition of the Senate, and government control of the export grain trade. They had professed a lack of faith in the old political parties, tied too closely,

E. A. Partridge

it was affirmed, to interests in Toronto and Montreal. Now T. A. Crerar, a farmer from Manitoba, former head of the Grain Growers' Grain Company, and a cabinet minister in the Union government, left the government to form a separate group, the Progressive party, which would fight elections on a farmers' platform.

Farmer candidates did well in the federal election of 1921. A total of sixty-five were elected across Canada, with Saskatchewan electing fourteen of a possible fifteen, and her sister prairie provinces doing almost as well. The Progressives found themselves to be the second largest party, numerically, in the House of Commons and were expected to assume the responsibility of official opposition. The party was divided internally, however, and could not agree on a course of action. It held the balance of power after both the 1921 and the 1925 elections, but its strength began to decline after the Alberta contingent broke away to form the United Farmers of Alberta "Ginger Group." Many Saskatchewan and Manitoba Progressives returned to their former party allegiance

7

as Liberal-Progressives. After the 1926 election, which was won by W. L. Mackenzie King, only a handful of Progressives remained.

Provincially, in Saskatchewan, the Progressives had had little success. The Liberals maintained a firm grip on the farm vote and exercised a restraining influence on the SGGA. This alienated many farmers who had worked hard to enunciate the farmers' platform. Out of their dissatisfaction came a new farm organization, the Farmers' Union of Canada, which had its beginning in Ituna late in 1921. It was endorsed by farmers in the Kelvington area in 1922 and gained strong support thereafter in areas settled by Ukrainian, German, and Scandinavian families. The SGGA had found its greatest strength along the main line of the CPR and in the long-settled areas of the province. The areas to the north had been almost neglected. By 1923 the new union was challenging the older organization for recognition as the real voice of organized farmers in the province.

The decline of the Progressives and the growth of the Farmers' Union were indicative of a shift in the farm movements' strategy. Direct political action had lost its appeal and,

while there was no lessening of unrest, this discontent now manifested itself in a renewed interest in the economic sphere. Farmers began to discuss the feasibility of handling and selling grain for themselves. They considered such action while the bumper crop of 1923 was being sold, by the private-sector machinery, at a price below the cost of production. It was obvious that neither the Saskatchewan Co-operative Elevator Company nor its counterpart in Alberta and Manitoba, the United Grain Growers, was able to increase the basic level of grain prices since they had little weight in the marketplace where grain was sold to international buyers. All this left fertile ground for the proponents of a "wheat pool," in which producers would pool their grain and handle and sell it themselves.

This was not an entirely new idea. Ed Partridge had advocated it as early as 1906. The Canadian Wheat Board had operated on a similar principle, applying a policy whereby all farmers received the same price for a certain grade of wheat, the price being the average received for the grade when it was sold. Many farmers argued that if the government would not control marketing, then farmers should

8

Saskatchewan Progressive Party executive, 1919 (B4190).

formally contract to sell their grain to a central pool. This would permit pool management to ascertain the probable volume of grain that would be available for sale and give them some control over contracted wheat supplies. The SGGA, however, opted for a temporary, voluntary, non-contract pool for the 1923 crop. Farmers began to take sides on the contract issue.

This was the situation when Aaron Sapiro agreed to visit Saskatchewan. He was a San Franciscan who had made a study of cooperative development in the Scandinavian countries and had returned to organize marketing co-operatives in Kentucky, where tobacco growers were in trouble, and in California, where citrus fruit growers were being exploited. It was reported that Sapiro's ideas were gaining support south of the border. He himself was said to be a forceful speaker and a good organizer. In 1923, the Farmers' Union invited Aaron Sapiro to come to Saskatchewan.

He delivered his first address in Saskatoon on August 23 of that year. He was forthright in his approach, and he spoke with conviction. It was not enough, he said, to have a farmers' union pooling grain, or a grain growers' association pooling grain, or even a government pooling grain. The real answer was to have a unified farm movement pooling grain. As a result of his persuasive oratory, officials from interested organizations met and agreed to form a Saskatchewan contract wheat pool for 1923. Indicative of the cooperative spirit engendered was the decision of the Saskatchewan Co-operative Elevator Company to put its resources behind the campaign for members.

Sapiro had cautioned farmers that a pool could not function effectively unless fifty-one percent of the wheat acreage was contracted for. This meant that a total of 6,100,000 acres had to be signed up before the time came to market the 1923 crop. By mid-September it was apparent that the goal could not be reached in so limited a time. Alberta farmers, fired by

Aaron Sapiro, 1927 (Saskatchewan Wheat Pool Collection, Saskatchewan Archives Board, A15,263).

Original pile of
Saskatchewan Wheat Pool
contracts. From left: George
W. Robertson, R. B. Ivans,
F. Pragnall, A. E. Wilson,
A. J. McPhail c. 1924
(B4188).

Sapiro with the same enthusiasm, came close to the fifty-one percent goal and organized the Alberta Wheat Pool. Saskatchewan farmers decided to let the issue rest before the public all winter and to recommence a sign-up campaign the following spring.

It was probably a wise decision, if for no other reason than it provided time for a thorough airing of the pooling concept. The topic was never far from the dinner table, the community hall, the livery stable, or the barbershop. The daily press in Regina and Saskatoon came out strongly in opposition. It took the threat of a libel action to moderate the editorial tone of one daily. With the coming of spring there was a rush to sign up members for the pool. Aaron Sapiro was invited back — and he came. Farmers, farm women, sons, and daughters helped persuade neighbors to join. In June, 1924 the goal was reached, and the decision was made to form the Saskatchewan Wheat Pool. A board of directors, meeting in July, elected A. J. McPhail as president and L. C. Brouillette as vice-president. George Robinson, an able farmer, was appointed secretary. That same month, the three prairie wheat pools — Manitoba had also formed a pool in 1924 — set up the Canadian Co-operative Wheat Producers Ltd. It was better known as the Central Selling Agency and was responsible only for sales of wheat. A. J. McPhail was elected the first president.

These arrangements took care of selling the wheat. Now, provision had to be made for receiving the wheat from the producers. The Saskatchewan Wheat Pool made arrangements with the existing elevator companies to handle the intake of the 1924 crop. At the same time the company set out to acquire its own elevators. It had 89 of its own ready for 1925 and then, in 1926, purchased the Saskatchewan Co-operative Elevator Company with its 451 country elevators and 4 terminal elevators. This put the Pool in a very strong position. By 1928-1929 there were 970 elevators in operation and a membership roll showing upwards of 80,000 members.

The Pool adopted the earlier, wheat-board policy of paying initial, interim, and final payments. This satisfied the growers, who received cash on delivery and further cash the following spring, when the previous year's crop was normally sold. It also permitted the Central Selling Agency to hold off wheat when the market was slow and sell when demand was brisk. This system gave farmers the assurance of a fair and equal price for all growers no matter when the grain was sold. It did have the drawback that the Pool had to draw on credit from financial houses at harvesttime, in order to make initial payments, but this posed few problems when economic conditions were good. The Central Selling Agency quickly learned the art of marketing, and the Wheat Pools brought some stability to the wheat market and a more orderly flow of grain at delivery points.

The Saskatchewan Wheat Pool had a marked social impact in addition to its economic role. Pool organization reached into every rural

Saskatchewan Wheat Pool, first general meeting of delegates, February, 1925. (B2922).

11

district as local committees were set up to debate issues and to promote renewals of membership. The province was divided into sixteen districts, with each district further divided into ten sub-districts. Each sub-district elected a delegate who attended and voted at the Pool's annual conventions. The ten delegates from each district elected one of their number to the Pool's board of directors. This body, in turn, elected the president from among its membership. Since the contract signed by each member at the farm level called for delivery of all that member's wheat delivered for sale, it was decided that the small farmer should have as much voting power as the big farmer. Since delegates were elected locally, the lists of members and delegates read like a list of people attending an international conference. Ukrainian, German, Scandinavian and Anglo-Saxon names were proof that the Pool brought "old" and "new" Canadians into the community of economic democracy.

The organization of the Pool was the lively evidence of a deep-felt need by farmers to do things for themselves and thus to shape their own destinies. The success of this cooperative venture sparked activity in other fields. A number of pools were organized for the selling of other agricultural products. Consumer cooperatives, which had begun on a small scale in the pioneer days, flourished now as well. The Saskatchewan government encouraged the development of cooperative enterprises, and all politicial parties had members who were cooperators. Saskatchewan became noted as the home of the cooperative ideal.

Almost without warning, modern Saskatchewan society had emerged by the late twenties. The land had filled up. Cities had blossomed to become centers of culture in addition to being centers of commerce. The automobile, airplane, and radio had lessened the isolation of prairie dwellers. On the farm, the homestead shack had given way to the two-storey frame home. The tractor had begun to supplant the workhorse. Saskatchewan youth boasted that, given a pair of pliers and a few yards of bailing wire, they could repair the world. Farmers' Union rallies, Wheat Pool meetings, mission circles, country dances, and sports days drew the varied ethnic strains together, as the young of the rising generation met each other on equal terms. The world seemed wide and good in those halcyon days.

Then, suddenly, out of nowhere, a dark cloud of dust and depression settled over the West. There had been economic setbacks before the market crash of late 1929, but the thirties brought economic disaster to the prairies. It was unrelenting, a series of misfortunes beyond the comprehension or control of political or economic man. Saskatchewan suffered a more severe blow than any other province in Canada. Thousands of farmers in the arid Palliser triangle were uprooted, blown out, to seek a new rooting in the north. Taxes went unpaid. Mortgages on farm land and farm implements were foreclosed. The Wheat Pool, the greatest cooperative enterprise yet built, suffered a staggering blow. It was forced to turn to governments for guarantees to cover loans that had been incurred in making initial payments on the 1929 crop. The price for such guarantees was the abandonment of its wheat-marketing activities to the federal government. The Saskatchewan Wheat Pool reverted to being a grain-handling enterprise. But it accepted the straitened role with courage, concentrating on paying off its debts, holding public meetings, and providing reading materials in rural areas. Library services were widely used as people everywhere, in town and country, questioned the "why" of the present and began to consider restructuring a society that had so betrayed them.

The people of Saskatchewan were indelibly marked by the experience of the thirties. The economic suffering of that decade provoked them into a renewed revolt against the commercial and financial institutions of central Canada. New political parties, dedicated to changing the system, were organized. The persistent concept of a cooperative commonwealth, rooted and grew anew, in a movement that took form as the Co-operative Commonwealth Federation. Leaders such as M. J. Coldwell, T. C. Douglas, Fred Williams, and Louise Lucas came to the fore. The cooperative oil refinery in Regina built with farmer dollars, proved that the will to cooperate was still strong. At the same time, under the leadership of the Dominion government, plans to rehabiliate the drought-stricken areas took shape. New machinery and new methods of farming, new laws to encourage conservation, to promote crop insurance, to stimulate research came into effect. Strip farming, trash cover, shelterbelts came into common parlance. By 1937, the worst year of all, Saskatchewan people had begun to fight back, to counter the ravages of wind and dust, to lay plans for a new society which would ensure that such want and poverty would not again stalk the prairie land.

The dirty thirties ended in the feverish activity of a world at war. Demand for resources — including foodstuffs — was high, and even with the end of hostilies there was no economic slump. Saskatchewan farmers prospered as the demand for food continued strong. But the province's industrial development had as yet received little stimulus, and young people drifted away as the mechanization of agriculture proceeded apace and the cities failed to provide jobs. Only when developments in oil, potash, and pulpwood attracted money and markets was the trend reversed. Then, people came back to share in a promised economic boom. Governments emphasized rural electrification, grid roads, regional libraries, and aid to local business and industry in an effort to preserve the sense of community and the social values rooted in small-town and rural Saskatchewan.

Saskatchewan, today, is a province unique. Yet neither geography nor history took special pains to form or nurture it. Certainly environment played a dominant role in determining the course of early settlement — but high skies, sun, wind, extremes of climate, scarcity of rain are shared with the other prairie provinces. It is the Saskatchewan people, their sense of community, that make the difference. Thus, there has developed in this province an infrastructure that binds the various levels of government to the people's wishes. Local government, cooperatives, and credit unions have provided a live and lively laboratory in the arts of governing and management. Regional parks and lake resorts invite family participation. The larger cities do not dominate social life and mores.

There is also about this province a sense of stability, of common sense, of cautious reflection. In Saskatchewan, wheat runs through all politics and policies. It is the mark of a Saskatchewan person that if you meet him in far away places he does not ask you about oil or potash or pulp — invariably his question is, "How are crops back home?" The Saskatchewan farmer buys in a protected market but must sell on a world market. He raises his product in a semiarid region with a highly unpredictable annual rainfall. Small wonder he searches for stability in the marketplace and protection from sudden misfortune. Medicare, government ownership, and cooperative ventures have been amongst the results.

It is true, of course, that not everyone in Saskatchewan supported the development of cooperatives. Not everyone shared the ideal of a cooperative commonwealth. Not every farmer supported the Wheat Pool or other marketing co-ops. Some preferred to think of themselves as independent entrepreneurs shaping each his own destiny. Hence we have "Ma" and "Dad" berating the cooperatives for driving independents out of business. Their conversation takes on political overtones, as they associate the New Democratic Party (successor to the CCF) with the support of co-ops. But their arguments lose force as son Louis illustrates how private business makes paper profits out of paper wheat before the loaf of bread appears on the table. And as Ma and Dad talk of their trip to Phoenix, the message is obvious — it is hard to appreciate the cooperative ideal in affluent times, for cooperation must be learned and the greatest teacher of all is necessity.

At what price, then, our prosperity? For the sod buster at the end of the play, the answer is clear: "I'd give it all to be young again. To hold my hands on the handles of a plough. To smell the warm earth and see it fall aside in waves, right to each side, smooth as water. I'd give it all to be young again and feel that I could change the world."

Dust storm — hills of potatoes, 1930s (A3523).

13

Paper Wheat:
Epic Theatre in Saskatchewan

Paper Wheat:
Epic Theatre in Saskatchewan

Don Kerr

Paper Wheat was a phenomenal Canadian theatrical success, as successful as almost any play in the country's history. It toured over eighty Canadian communities, played over 200 performances, and was seen by 65,000 people. It was televised by CBC and its second tour filmed by the National Film Board. Almost every review of *Paper Wheat* was enthusiastic and almost every audience even more enthusiastic. Standing ovations became a matter of course as audience after audience found themselves intensely drawn to the play. A letter from Saskatoon gave the best short account of the play's effect on people: "I laughed, I cried, and understood."

Yet *Paper Wheat* only got staged by the skin of its teeth by a theatre company, 25th Street Theatre in Saskatoon, that had been surviving for years by the skin of its teeth. The story of how the company made the play happen is not unlike a homesteader proving up his quarter section in dry weather and needing a lot of help from his friends to survive.

1. The Production

The play opened in Sintaluta, Saskatchewan, on March 18, 1977. Sintaluta, population 200, was the home of Ed Partridge, one of the heroes of the farmers' movement featured in the play. Opening night was tense. An hour before curtain time director and actors were still arguing over the last scene. The play was a bit formless and uncertain and the actors were scared. As the audience began to file into the Memorial Hall, a car pulled up outside with the backdrop strapped on top. A friend, Aiden Beck, had stayed up all night to paint it and had then driven down from Saskatoon. A fellow in the audience told them there were blankets in the basement they could use for backing. The

play began a few minutes late. After each scene the actors checked a list pinned up back stage to see what scene came next — they had never had a complete run through of the play before opening night. And many of the scenes never made it to a second night, including a ten minute opening on the origin of mankind.

Layne Coleman, an important member of the theatre company, was in the audience that night and had to stand at the back because the hall was so full. There were scenes he couldn't understand and others so embarrassing he hid in the cloakroom until they were over. In one scene a man's wife died because he was too cheap to get a doctor and at the end he was rocking his baby which was a bundle of sheets. The audience laughed and the company had succeeded in reducing tragedy to vaudeville. In one of the good scenes a farmer proposed marriage to his hired girl. Bob Bainborough was playing the farmer and the scene opened with the girl telling him to take off his muddy shoes when he comes into the house. On opening night one of Bainborough's shoes was knotted and wouldn't come off. He had to walk in with one shoe on and one shoe off, saying "Well, this is the clean shoe." For director Andy Tahn the low point came when Michael Fahey expressed the joy of being on the prairie by exclaiming, "Look at the wheat sheaves growing out of my hair," and making hand gestures to match. Tahn winced. What will a farm audience think of that? That's it then, the theatre company is dead.

Were they finally down to their last bootstrap? But the audience thought the scene was funny on purpose and laughed. It was a long night and the play finally ended at eleven. The actors are old people at the end, remembering, and the last line was spoken: "I'd give it all to be young again and feel that I could change the

world." The audience was moved and stood and cheered and cheered. Bainborough couldn't believe the reaction. It was "a magic moment." That was the first and most important of many standing ovations for *Paper Wheat*. Coleman, Tahn, Bainborough all think that without that exciting opening night response there would be no *Paper Wheat* story to tell.

By the second night, in Moose Jaw, the play had been cut and pasted and a large new sequence in which Grain Growers' Gertie wrestles Big Business Bertha added to put more history into the play. Only thirteen people showed up. The company then ran what amounted to its dress rehearsal in Regina, to mixed response. There were a couple of standing ovations but there also seemed to be a strong anti-co-op feeling in the city and the play received a bad review. There was a successful performance in Eston, where much of the play had been put together, and the news account noted one of the special charms the play had for rural Saskatchewan — it reminded some of "good old musical gatherings." By the time the company opened in Saskatoon *Paper Wheat* had been tightened and polished. It played to two weeks of sold out houses with standing ovations almost every night and a highly favorable review. The cast felt they had come home. The production was a success.

But it was a close thing. There is a scene early in Act One where a farmer and his wife fold and refold a blanket as they list the series of hardships that have met their best endeavors. That blanket folded and refolded could tell the story of 25th Street Theatre too. It was begun in

1972 by Andy Tahn and others, primarily recent university graduates, including two people who later played a part in the success of *Paper Wheat*, Sharon Bakker and Gerry Stoll. It has lived by hook and crook, grants and will power ever since.

Originally it operated as a kind of arts centre, published a literary magazine (two issues), founded a dance troupe and a band, and brought all the activities together in a performance of a script by Andy Tahn called *Covent Garden* in the Saskatoon Centennial Auditorium (seating capacity 2,000). It was a large failure, though one of the actors most identified with the theatre, Layne Coleman, was a dancer in the production. Theatre became the focus of the group in 1973 and they received one of the last federal government LIP (Local Initiatives Program) grants that were responsible for so many new theatres in Canada. In the next three years they did a Ken Mitchell premiere, *Pleasant Street*, Ken Campbell's *Pilk's Madhouse*, D. A. Murphy's *A Virus Called Clarence*. Tahn's version of *Billy the Kid* was the first sell out, in the spring of 1975, and the play that won them their first Canada Council grant. But it almost didn't make it. The theatre was broke, as it was after almost every production. Tahn said give me a weekend to have a script and in three days he did *Billy the Kid* with roles tailored for Layne Coleman and Bob Collins. Chris Covert directed and Don Freed wrote the music. Coleman's girlfriend came out from Montreal and a role was written into the play for her, as an historically non-existent girlfriend to Billy the Kid. That was Linda Griffiths who added so much energy to the first production of *Paper*

Wheat. Only five out of fifteen actors were paid on *Billy the Kid* as the company used up another bootstrap. In the fall Paul Thompson of Theatre Passe Muraille, Toronto, directed the company's first collective production, *If You're So Good Why Are You in Saskatoon,* also a success, as was another collective, *Unicorn,* with music by Steve Bengston and Ross Campbell. The company felt optimistic, unlike the usual year end. Coleman says ordinarily the company was ready to fold at the end of every season. "We'd get together for coffee with Andy and he would say, 'Well, what'll we do next year?' and someone would say something stupid and Andy would advertise it and we'd have to do it."

The 1976-77 season was advertised as the "blockbuster" season and the fifth show in the season was advertised as *The Co-op Show,* though not a line of the play had been written nor a strand of the plot thought out. Tahn wanted the company to get more deeply involved in Saskatchewan history.

Nor did the theatre have a home — each of the four plays finally produced was put on in a different auditorium, only one of which was a proper theatre. The second and third productions were failures and the theatre was again out of money. Tahn and the company had a meeting and everyone left town except Tahn and business manager Gerry Stoll. They then went around to hustle up money and got a number of small donations. The Board took out a loan as well. Tahn started phoning actors to form a collective production on the co-ops. Linda Griffiths came back from Toronto. Michael Fahey was hired when his roommate couldn't come, and Fahey brought his guitar

with him. It was the first major role for Bob Bainborough, while Catherine Jaxon and Brenda Leadlay had never been in professional theatre before. Tahn met Sharon Bakker in Vancouver. She had been with the company in the beginning but was now settled down and was out of theatre. She took a day to reply but said yes and by the end of the fourth tour was probably the best single performer in the play though competition for that spot was fierce.

The company that went out to create the Co-op show was largely innocent of Saskatchewan history. They didn't know the Wheat Pool from Cargill or even that the Wheat Pool was a cooperative. They didn't know the story was going to be a farmers' story or who the hero might be, or the villain. Albert Trew was one of many people Tahn brought in to talk to the cast. He'd been one of the founders of the Wheat Pool and in a very quiet way he talked about the early days, pointed the company towards the Pool and towards ordinary people as heroes of the story. When he finished his listeners were in tears, which the company would later transfer to thousands of others. The company, which began rehearsals February 5, went out to three areas of the province to develop their story, the Eston-Kyle area, the Cudworth-Wakaw area, and the Sintaluta-Wolesley area. In Eston they were able to use a farm home as headquarters through the kindness of the owners Mr. and Mrs. Gerald Thompson, and that was typical of the kindness they met almost everywhere.

When they got to a new town they would go to the cafe, ask if anyone knew people who could talk about the founding of the Pool.

19

Guy Sprung, director of *Paper Wheat* during the provincial and national tours.

They'd be told to talk to Charlie or Mrs. Johnstone and would go and have tea with them. Then at night they performed skits based on the day's material, ultimately creating over two hundred skits, out of which less than twenty survived. On one bad day when they'd run out of contacts Tahn sent them down different streets to knock on doors, like a travelling theatre company shopping for stories. When they weren't in Eston they had sometimes to rehearse in a car or a cafe or someone's basement.

Times weren't always good times and there was considerable pressure on the company, which was sometimes working sixteen hours a day on a subject which was larger than they expected and which they had to bring into focus. Only Linda Griffiths and Andy Tahn had done collective theatre before and it was an exciting but unnerving way to work. Actors were now both writers and actors and what went wrong was entirely their responsibility. Sometimes there was no creativity at all, or invention could misfire and produce awful results, some of which were staged opening night. Coleman says it's a process where you look at your own mediocrity every day. For an actor it means living dangerously, trial by fire, and it is addictive. Tahn pushed the cast and they pushed back.

Slowly the play began to focus, first as a story about farmers and early co-ops rather than the retail cooperative movement, then as a story about the Wheat Pool. Tahn knew early on from his reading that Ed Partridge had to be part of the story and thus the decision to do research in the Sintaluta area. In one of his skits Michael Fahey used the expression "paper wheat" — there was a pause and the words

clicked. It took a bit of time to throw out other provisional titles, like "Hewers of Wood and Drawers of Water," but once the title was chosen that helped focus the play too. Partridge and the Winnipeg Grain Exchange became even more central, though in the first version of the play the term "paper wheat" was inadequately explained, because, Andy Tahn says, they didn't fully understand it. The politics were a kind of by-product of the search for a co-op story. When the company found their story they found the politics already inside it, though most of them when they started were as innocent of agrarian politics as they had been of Saskatchewan history. Ollie Turnbull of the Co-op College helped them to understand a historic structure within which the company created their story.

The process of collective creation was a complex one. Out of one of the daily exercises came the great song in Act One, Bob Bainborough's "Bessie." Linda Griffiths contributed the very last speech so important to the play's impact. Sharon Bakker created her male elevator agent. And so on. Though individuals created this or that character or speech, the play was a collective creation and collective theatre could sometimes work marvellously. But it has inherent difficulties — trying to find a form for the amorphous material coming in, trying to let everyone in the cast have their say on stage even when some inventions are better than others. As this play began to take shape there was the painful necessity of dropping good scenes because they were no longer important to the story, and including some less good scenes because they were necessary. According to Tahn, Bainborough and Griffiths were particularly important in the collective process because they invented the humor that gave the edge to so many of the scenes in the play.

Even though the first version of *Paper Wheat* remained a bit ungainly and confused in places, the heart of the play was there and the success story had begun. 25th Street Theatre had not had so close an acquaintance with success that they were going to let this one get away. Before the first tour was finished money for the second was being solicited. Because a couple of the actors wanted someone other than Tahn to direct the second tour he contacted Guy Sprung of Montreal to take it over. Tahn thought he had gone as far as he could with the material, and had been impressed with Sprung's production of David Fennario's *Nothing to Lose*. The two had been talking about a production of Tahn's *Jacob Kepp*, which became the great constant in 25th Street Theatre programs — it was four times advertised before being produced, successfully, in 1980. Sprung had been a co-founder of one of the best and most important of the London fringe theatres that came to life after 1968, the Half Moon Theatre in Aldgate. That theatre developed close ties with

Provincial touring cast, Fall 1977. Left to right, standing: David Francis, Sharon Bakker, Skai Leja, Lubomir Mykytiuk, Richard Rinder (Technician), Lynne Hostein (Stage Manager); kneeling: fiddler Bill Prokopchuk, Michael Fahey.

the community, performing plays written by and about the area, and like so many fringe theatres in Britain it was also left wing. Sprung could feel at home with a community drama that celebrated a cooperative victory.

Only two actors from the first cast, Bakker and Fahey, were available for the second tour and Sprung brought three new actors with him, David Francis, Lubomir Mykytiuk, and Skai Leja. The new balance of three male and two female actors made better sense than the original cast of four women and two men, but then Sprung had more money and less pressure which assisted his choices. For his sixth performer Sprung wanted a fiddle player and Tahn got Bill Prokopchuk to join the cast. An experienced old time fiddler from the Yorkton area Prokopchuk added more than his music to the play. He wasn't a young actor come in to tell people their story but looked like a participant in the story and clearly came from its world. So he added a new kind of bond between the play and its audiences. Not that there seemed to be any resentment against young people or outsiders doing a local story. Letters and reviews were happy that the young wanted to learn and tell the story of their grandparents' generation.

Sprung and his new cast built on the first version of *Paper Wheat* but changed it considerably too, mostly for the better. Act One was given a sharper form by having the ethnic cross section of the first version reduced to five characters, one for each actor. In Act Two the chronology was made clearer, the politics stronger, and there was some attempt to bring the story down to the present. Louise Lucas represented the thirties and a contemporary farm family was added. In their wake came Cargill, conglomerates and the present economic returns to the farmer from a loaf of bread. Lubomir Mykytiuk in particular added a great deal to the play. His Ukrainian in Act One, his quiet performance as Ed Partridge and the nightly show stopper, his juggling act, were all strikingly good. Skai Leja was the best singer to perform in the play. David Francis was as good as Bob Bainborough had been, which was very good. Version two missed the brightness of Linda Griffiths, especially in Act One.

The second tour began in Saskatoon, September 27, 1977 playing two weeks there, then a week in Toronto, followed by thirty-three one night stands in Saskatchewan communities; the most extensive theatre tour in the province's history. It was also performed for a Wheat Pool convention and an NDP convention. Albert Kish of the NFB saw a videotaped version of the play in Toronto and came out to watch it at Assiniboia. "I never saw responses to theatre like I saw in the Saskatchewan towns, night after night." He organized NFB participation almost at once through the *Challenge for Change* series, and a crew followed the last thirteen dates on the tour, from Strasbourg to Central Butte (including Sintaluta). The $160,000 film, released in 1979, is a marvellous record of the play and its audience. The response in Saskatchewan to the play was again immensely enthusiastic. This comment from Rosetown was typical: "It was very close in the Community Hall by the end of the performance, but I don't think a single person, young or old, felt the heat. They were too busy reliving or discovering a heritage; our heritage, Saskatchewan's heritage." One lady who had been in the cooperative struggle described by the play showed an insider's appreciation: "I loved the reference to patronage dividends." But if the play worked for the people who recognized their past in it, how would it work in the rest of Canada?

That's the question tour three answered. Tour three was substantially a repeat of the second tour. With the exception of Michael Fahey the cast remained the same, while the play, again under the direction of Guy Sprung, remained basically the same. It was a bit longer and a bit better dressed, but though more elaborate props and costumes gave a professional veneer to the play they also took away from the simplicity of the first version and the sense of the actors having made do with their own resources. The play began as a quarter section homesteader; by its third tour it owned a section of good land.

The tour opened in Calgary and played Alberta in June and July to sold-out houses and audiences as enthusiastic as any. There were two weeks in Saskatchewan before *Paper Wheat* opened the season at the National Theatre Centre in Ottawa. Then came three weeks in Vancouver in September, a series of performances in Southern Ontario in October and two week stands in November in Montreal and Toronto.

Fears that the play might not work outside its own backyard were soon proved unfounded. *Paper Wheat* travelled well. The audience at the National Arts Centre in Ottawa were equal to that at Sintaluta and gave the play a standing ovation on opening night. One reviewer was reluctant at first. "At first glance, the early struggles of a farmers' cooperative and the creation of the Saskatchewan Wheat Pool don't appear a very promising subject for an evening's entertainment." For another the attempt to stay outside the play to watch and analyze it failed. "You may want to retain a certain degree of distance, a remoteness from the events but you find yourself charmed by the participants. . . ." That comment helps make clear both the degree to which audiences were drawn into the play and the extent to which the performance of *Paper Wheat,* aside from the text, made it a success.

Not all responses to the play were positive. There were a few attacks on the play as a commercial message for the Wheat Pool or as a play unfair to free enterprise, but those attacks never analyzed the play itself. For instance, an editorial in the *Free Press Report on Farming*

attacked the play for perpetuating a myth that has divided farmers and industry for fifty years; that the play's message is irrelevant to modern agriculture, and that it derides "a barely functioning futures market." Someday all parts of the grain industry will work together, says the editorial, but until then we will have to suffer the "theatre of the absurd." The attack might have substance except that the editorialist hadn't seen the play but only read of it. There were also attacks from the left, usually on the inadequate history of Act Two, attacks of some substance that we will deal with later. Some reviewers while enjoying the production found the play thin, but only one, Martin Knelman in *Saturday Night,* decided the thing was entirely wrong-headed from beginning to end. He attacked with obvious relish "rural folksiness," "yokel gags," and "simple peasant traditions," and particularly objected to what he considered the false, sentimental nobility of the western peasants, and offered his own brand of heretical urban sophistication as a relief to the moral earnestness that infected *Paper Wheat,* the CBC, the NFB, and Canada Council. Knelman would not have gone down well in Sintaluta.

Virtually everyone liked *Paper Wheat.* Its success depended on a good text, a good cast, a special rapport with its audience. It also depended on money, business energy, and nerve. Tahn, Stoll and others made the play keep happening. The first tour depended on Tahn and Stoll begging for money on the basis of a play that didn't yet have a line of text. That first rehearsal and tour cost $17,000. The box office returned $4,500, Saskatchewan Culture and Youth gave $2,000, the Canada Council Touring Office $1,000, the cooperative movement $1,500 (after the performances had begun); the rest of the money was made up out of annual grants and smaller personal contributions. The cast received less than equity for the tour. The 1977 fall tour of Saskatchewan, organized town by town by the theatre, cost $65,000, half of which was recouped at the box office. The Canada Council Touring Office provided $10,000, the Wheat Pool $8,000, the Credit Union and other co-ops $6,000, Saskatchewan Culture and Youth $7,000. The national tour in 1979 was the big one and cost over $210,000, two thirds of which was recouped from the box office. Even with success things didn't come easy and the tour was almost cancelled. In the summer the tour was partly booked but there were still long gaps between some dates. Canada Council gave 25th Street House Theatre a deadline — book the rest of the Alberta dates in ten days or lose the Canada Council money. When Julie Krause applied for a job as manager with the theatre Tahn decided to test her. He gave her the keys to a rented car and off she went to Alberta, keeping in touch with Tahn by phone. She booked the tour and got the job. The Canada Council Touring Office contributed $30,000 this time, Saskatchewan Sports Trust $36,000, and the Wheat Pool and the Department of Cooperation $20,000. There are three conclusions to be drawn from these figures: the need for subsidies for even the most successful theatre, the importance of the Canada Council to the well-being of *Paper Wheat*, and the important but relatively modest contributions made by the cooperative movement. The play was not a kept play. Federated Cooperatives subsequently very handsomely funded the sequel to *Paper Wheat, Generation and 1/2,* to help celebrate its 50th Anniversary.

2. The Genealogy

When *Paper Wheat* was performed in small Western towns it was playing for the most part to people who had little experience with live theatre. Yet its form, so surprising from some points of view, was not that remote from the experience of older members of that audience. The play is a little like a Christmas concert or an amateur hour, in which skit follows skit and all the actors take a turn doing their number, singing their song or delivering their monologue. It's put together with simple props too, the way a high school play might be. The stage is generally bare except for a few chairs and a table. A blanket represents hard times, a bun juggled and eaten bit by bit becomes the economic returns from grain farming. Everyone, whether new to theatre or not, can see how the thing works. In fact, once you've seen a play like *Paper Wheat* nothing seems more obvious than putting plays together that way, as a series of episodes that tell a story, and mixing together whatever the story needs: mixing all the arts — mime, song, dance, dialogue, oratory; mixing literary genres — comedy and tragedy, the domestic and the heroic; doing, in fact, whatever is necessary to tell the story.

Once we've seen a play like *Paper Wheat* the style may seem ovious and simple, but such theatre came to birth with some difficulty, and 25th Street Theatre built its success upon the work of important predecessors. The dominant kind of theatre in the past hundred years has been Realism and it was invented primarily by Henrik Ibsen in the 1870's and 80's. Ibsen said he wanted his plays to give "the illusion of reality." He wanted members of his audience to believe that what they saw in theatre was actually happening, to forget in fact that they were in a theatre. The room on stage has simply had its fourth wall removed and we in the audience are privileged to eavesdrop on life itself. Settings were usually detailed interiors, characters more often than not members of the middle class that became the theatre goers for this kind of serious drama. The new social sciences, sociology and psychology, often

fought for pre-eminence in the plays or blended their insights, and characters were complex creations set in complex surroundings like Ibsen's Hedda Gabler, or Osborne's Jimmy Porter, or Albee's George and Martha. They were rounded characters with a full biography and with fears and hopes, vice and virtue mixed. In fact, as the audience was brought to see more and more deeply into the human psyche, words like vice and virtue began to seem antiquated. The theatre that Realism replaced, melodrama and romance, seemed particularly old-fashioned and irrelevant with their stereotyped and simple characters and stories and their extrovert, broad theatrical style. There have been many permutations in the history of Realism, but it still remains the dominant mode of performed story telling today, in great part because of the camera which can trace external reality in such detail. Realism is the natural mode for cinema and television.

Among a number of theatrical revolts against Realism in this century, the one that leads to *Paper Wheat* was best formulated by German dramatist Bertolt Brecht. Beginning in the 1920's Brecht developed a theory and practice he called epic theatre as opposed to what he called dramatic theatre, which included Realism. In the dramatic mode a story was a seamless continuum; events flowed naturally and invisibly into one another. Characters seemed to have little control over events and fate to control their destinies. Brecht said he wanted a theatre that would not reflect reality but lead to "the mastering of reality." He wanted to show the world as alterable and man as able to alter himself and the world. Ed Partridge's view of politics in *Paper Wheat* is close to Brecht's view of the function of theatre.

Epic theatre was composed of episodes, each clearly divided from the others so that the continuum is broken. The ordinary means of theatrical illusion — lighting effects, scenery — were to be openly manipulated so that an audience was aware of theatre and therefore less likely to confuse art with reality. Actors were to quote only those parts of a character necessary for a scene and not become the character, not identify heart and soul with a character. Brecht said the epic play could fully use all emotions but one — the special empathy between actor and audience by which the audience becomes lost in one point of view and so becomes the willing and blind accomplice of whatever view the dramatist is promulgating. If we walk blind how can we alter the world? For Brecht the text is not sacred but, like life, is open to alteration.

One can quickly see points in common between Brechtian theory and *Paper Wheat*. The play is episodic. It constantly reminds us we're at a theatre, and while Lubomir Myky-

Sharon Bakker feeding chickens — "His Grain Is Just a Little Bit Better".

tiuk's juggling act is the epitome of showmanship in the play, partly because we don't expect a circus act in drama, in a way all the performances are like the juggling act, and audiences appreciate both the story *and* the way it is done. They are aware of the skills, partly because of the device of actors changing roles, and so have both an aesthetic response and an emotional response. Realism cannot play for so overt an aesthetic response because that would subvert "the illusion of reality." In *Paper Wheat* characterization is not psychological or complex, but only as complex as the idea of a scene demands. For instance, the elevator agent must plausibly cheat the Irish farmer and Sean has first to hope for the best and then get furious. The point of the scene is not to make Sean and the agent as much like full, complex human

beings as possible, but to illustrate with liveliness and clarity one of the turn-of-the-century swindles that inspired the forming of the Grain Growers' Grain Company. The theme of *Paper Wheat,* as expressed in the last line, and Brecht's theme, are the same; that men and women can alter the world.

Ibsen could not have told a story about the founding of the Wheat Pool. Such a broad historic sweep is not open to Realism. Ibsen could focus on a character like Ed Partridge, choose a crucial period in his life to explore, and dramatize, for instance, his will to power and the cost he or his family had to pay for his advocacy. A complex man would be created within a complex environment and time and place would be circumscribed. Brechtian theatre could tell the story of the founding of the Wheat Pool, though in fact Brecht's own plays never attempted close historical accuracy but operated more often as parables, like the *Paper Wheat* of Act One. Brecht was, however, involved in the 1920's German theatre of Erwin Piscator which did choose specific historic themes for presentation — origins of the Russian Revolution, the exploitation of resources in the Balkans, the origins of inflation.

Brecht's plays were not collective creations as was *Paper Wheat.* In Britain the theatre that pioneered collective creation was Joan Littlewood's Theatre Workshop at Stratford East, London, and that company's most famous collective creation was *Oh What A Lovely War,* done in 1963. It was a historical, musical, comic, tragic account of World War I and the greatest performance I've seen. Actors in the company eventually became writers and directors in the company, as have some at 25th Street Theatre. The direct connection between Theatre Workshop, London and Canadian drama is George Luscombe, founder of Toronto Workshop Production, who worked in the Littlewood company in the fifties and whose production of *Ten Lost Years,* based on Barry Broadfoot's oral history of the depression, toured Canada in 1974. It was the first play performed in Saskatoon in the style that *Paper Wheat* would follow. Props were few, actors played many roles, all the modes of theatre were used — music, mime, dialogue. The play was a series of episodes that defined the Canadian depression, and its hero was a group, the victims of the depression, rather than an individual man or woman. Group as hero is characteristic of collective theatre. In *Oh What A Lovely War* the "hero" is the men in the trenches in the Great War and in *Paper Wheat* it is the farmers. The collective mode of creation may help influence that outcome, especially when the story is based on interviews with people.

The most famous Canadian collective creation was Theatre Passe Muraille's *The Farm*

Show. The Toronto-based company visited Clinton, Ontario, talked to the farming community there and made a play out of that research which they first staged at Clinton in 1972. The Canadian prototype for *Paper Wheat* existed then just as 25th Street Theatre was beginning to find its legs in Saskatoon. A key date in this theatrical genealogy is 1975, the year Passe Muraille, under director Paul Thompson, came to Saskatchewan to create a collective play on the province. *The West Show* was a seven episode version of Saskatchewan history, starting with the Riel Rebellion and ending with the Farmers' Union tractor demonstration against Trudeau in 1968. The play opened in Rosthern and played some thirty Saskatchewan communities (including Sintaluta). It was a marvellous text and a marvellous production, as good as *Paper Wheat,* but the play has never been published and is largely forgotten, in great part I think because Passe Muraille was an established theatre with other projects already mapped out while 25th Street Theatre was hungry for success, and survival, and made its success continue to happen. Out of adversity, success. While doing *The West Show* Thompson also directed the 25th Street Theatre's first collective, *If You're so Good Why Are You in Saskatoon,* and the genealogy of *Paper Wheat* is complete.

3. The Text

The text of *Paper Wheat* in this book is the third version of the play. Version one is the play as created by Andy Tahn and the first cast. Version two is the play as revised by Guy Sprung and the second cast, and the revisions were considerable. It is the play that went on the national tour and was published in *Canadian Theatre Review,* Winter, 1978. Version three is Tahn's slightly edited version of the second *Paper Wheat.*

All three versions retain the basic distinction between Act One and Act Two. Act One is a series of short parables that feature fictional characters. Act Two is based on history and presents 'real' people like Ed Partridge and is based on actual events — the rise of the Grain Growers' and the Wheat Pool. That division between two very different kinds of play was important to *Paper Wheat*'s success because it lent such variety to the play. In the first version of Act One there were twelve characters representing the new settlers to the West, some of whom appeared in more than one sequence; in particular a Scottish woman and two English couples. There was also a German lady, a Norwegian, and very briefly, a Ukrainian farmer. The scenes central to Act One in all three versions were created by the first cast: "Squeezing the Land", "Marriage Proposal", "Old Bessie," and the sequence with the elevator agent. Guy Sprung and the second cast

made three kinds of changes to the act. They tightened some of the individual scenes — for instance, "Exercise" is now one-quarter its original length. They reduced the number of settlers to five — one for each actor — and organized all scenes around those five. That entailed some losses — Michael Fahey's Norwegian was even more fun than his Irishman in the contest with the elevator agent. And it entailed more gains, especially Lubomir Mykytiuk's Vasil. Finally, the second cast rewrote the beginning of the play to introduce their new characters and rearranged the sequence of events. They made one mistake, I think, in placing "Squeezing the Land" so early in the act before it is sufficiently prepared for. Tahn has made only two changes for this edition. His version of "Smells" is closer to the original, which was more visceral, and a mimed sequence, "Stuck in the Mud," created for the second version has been dropped. Thematically it was a repeat of scenes with the broken plough and the stubborn oxen, so little has been lost.

The sequence of events in Act One is quite complicated and there is no reason why a new cast might not rework or reorder some of the material again. The act opens with a touch of the politics that is central to Act Two in the song on the National Dream and the scene with the crooked storekeeper. We forget social protest in the scenes that follow. The first half of the act is not about cooperation at all but about settlement. The most powerful sequence in performance is "Squeezing the Land," about the farmer's battle with his first great enemy (and friend), nature. The play shifts to its central theme with the scene on the broken plough; one of the scenes considerably edited and much improved in Sprung's version and wonderfully acted by Bakker, Francis, and Mykytiuk. The rest of the scenes in the act work variations on cooperation. Even "Old Bessie" can be seen as a comic version of "un-cooperation". With the elevator agent and the farmers' anger we're prepared to move into the history of Act Two.

The changes in the three versions of Act Two are more wide-ranging and each version gives a different emphasis to the historical material. The original version had four major sequences: the wrestling match; the Partridge sequence, done in nine scenes and taking up two–thirds of the final act; the founding of the Wheat Pool; and the old people remembering. The chronology is 1905, 1924, and the present. The Partridge sequence is the centre of the act. In the present version of the play only the 1924 philosophical speech and poems are largely new. The original version also contains a scene with a comic aristocratic snob who laughs at uneducated farmers trying to think, and a political meeting where Partridge makes his report and which features a fight between two bull-headed farmers. That's both a nice reprise

Left to right: Bob Bainborough (as Partridge) and Sharon Hughes (as Motherwell) in "Organizing the Pool".

of the broken plough scene and a nice sour, humorous way for the co-op movement to start off. There are then a series of important short scenes in which we are shown a cross section of political attitudes and the cost the radical politician pays for his beliefs and leadership. In the meeting Partridge has already been contrasted with the more conservative Motherwell. Now he meets a woman who admires what he has done, an irate farmer who says he's sold both his ideals and patronage dividends. Partridge must defend the complexities of actual history and say the ideal is farther away than he realized. Now he is the politician who must live with actual events and not with dreams. To prove his honesty to us the next sequence has him refusing to sell the company to American interests. A friend then warns Ed that people are talking about him — they say he's both

politically ambitious for an Ottawa job and that he's too radical — they're calling him a Communist and atheist. Ed says I've my beliefs and they're common sense beliefs, but he decides to resign from the Grain Growers' Grain Company and let a more diplomatic man take over. The sequence is attractive partly because it has not precisely calculated what our response to it should be. By version two *Paper Wheat* is a very clear play which knows how an audience is to respond to almost every scene. The first Partridge sequence is more like an actual political meeting where we might want to argue after the passage is over about what it means and who was right and by how much.

However, if the Partridge sequence itself was more attractive in the first version the act as a whole was very unbalanced. I think the choice for Sprung and the second cast was either to give the whole act to Partridge or to reduce his impact and give a fuller coverage to later developments. Given the general theme of settlement and cooperation in Act One, Sprung's changes to the second act makes sense. There are five distinct sequences in the second version: the Partridge sequence, which still takes up one-quarter of the act; the founding of the Wheat Pool, which is roughly the same as in version one, though Aaron Sapiro has given way to Farmer Leo; a new bridging sequence for the 1930's — a speech by Louise Lucas; a new scene with a contemporary family; and the original version of the old people remembering. Sprung's version makes two substantial changes to the act. The original focus on founding the Wheat Pool gives way to the more general theme of cooperation, as stated in the Louise Lucas speech especially, but also comically in the contemporary family ("just a co-op minute") and in Partridge's philosophical reminiscence. The second version is also more overtly political than the original. The complex view of Partridge is replaced by one where we simply admire him; the radio scene where the Grain Exchange hires spies is added, though its political impact is muffled by its theatrical fun; Louise Lucas is new; most important is the contemporary family, where we meet Mr. Otto Gill, spokesman for Cargill, and then hear a bedtime story on Mr. Con Glomerate before exiting with the juggling version of the returns to the farmer from a loaf of bread. The second version also adds some of the most inventive short sequences to the play: the joining of the separate wheat sheaves into one co-operative wheat sheaf, the cooperative tap dance, and the juggling act.

A word about the politics in the second version. The additions look like socialism but socialist commentators have pointed out that *Paper Wheat* does not critically examine the co-op movement itself. It is easy to attack Mr. Con Glomerate but how does the Wheat Pool function in a capitalist marketplace? What have the farmers gained from their struggles years ago? In Sprung's version the capitalists today remain simple enemies to the good guys, the Wheat Pool, the cooperatives, and the farmer, and that fits the feeling of the play well enough, though for many it no longer fits their knowledge of the co-op movement. Yet a critical scene would hardly fit the play either. *Paper Wheat* is a celebration of a heroic age when men and women took on the world and won. It is not a play that tells the cost of radical politics. This time we get the party without the hangover. The torch of idealism is handed on to a new generation.

Tahn's version of the play, which you read here, is based on version two with some of the overt politics removed. Gone are Mr. Otto Gill and Mr. Con Glomerate. Their excising solves the political problem in a way — there is no longer any comment on contemporary history. That modern family scene now has only two parts to it; the comedy of the rich farm family surrounded by co-op products and the juggling

27

Skai Leja raises David Francis' hem in "Farmer Leo".

Lubomir Mykytiuk and Skai Leja from the chocolate cake scene in "Leo".

act which proves all the fights have to be fought again. That seems to me a successful concise version of modern farm 'history', though I still miss the Cargill man because that was the one scene in version two where our responses were not clearly planned for us. The Cargill speech was apparently a copy of an actual speech, so the company makes its own defence, which is plausible enough and not seriously argued down by the play, except by the general context. The conglomerate bedtime story on the other hand had almost no theatrical inventiveness and is best out. With the politics muted this version of the play is closer to what Tahn wanted in the first place, "a play about people." It also becomes more clearly a play about heroic endeavor.

The fact that there have been three versions of history in Act Two should be sufficient warning not to view the play as history. John Archer's history of the co-ops also makes the point clear. *Paper Wheat* is a highly selective view of agrarian history. One of its major functions indeed is to distill from history a simple and intense myth by which people today can still live; a myth of cooperation, of people able to alter the world. There are other stories in the material *Paper Wheat* is based on, and I will mention one to show how selective Act Two is and what raw material still awaits transformation into the literary myth. The CPR and the National Policy make a very brief appearance in the opening song and then disappear. There's not a Crow's Nest in sight, nor one freight rate, nor the dream of a Hudson Bay Railway. There's no farmers' political movement, and in particular the Progressive

Party which swept the West in 1921 is missing. Most remarkably there's not a single mention of the tariff. Take these topics out of the story and you remove one of the great Western agrarian themes — the regional revolt against eastern Canadian economic and political control. The theme makes a vestigial appearance in *Paper Wheat*, in the opening song and in Partridge's vision of a separate country in the West, though there was a stronger anti–eastern sentiment in his speech in the original *Paper Wheat*. The play is not less good because it chooses some themes and ignores others. But it is a play and not history and there are other plays to be written from the agrarian history of the West.

Why did *Paper Wheat* work so extraordinarily well? Because I think it successfully combined two opposite kinds of theatre art experience, which we can call Idealism and Realism. The story is like a fairy tale, yet we are convinced that it describes what actually happened. There is a great deal of hope in the story, yet that hope is grounded by scepticism. People win but they are rarely perfect. Farmer Leo is as typical as Louise Lucas. The story is heroic but it is also down to earth — it is about a great human venture, the settling of the West and the founding of a massive cooperative, yet we most often view that heroic adventure from a quarter section, or the kitchen, or the barber shop. Finally we constantly see the building of a new world through the perspective of comedy. *Paper Wheat* knows how to play to a popular audience yet it never played down to that audience. It is a very sophisticated piece of popular theatre, whose best scenes in performance were so rich and well done they could be enjoyed again and again.

Look at how the play transforms the founding of the Wheat Pool into theatre. The cast worked from a story that was heroic and victorious, which is the story they were told when they interviewed participants. The temptation to become sentimental and heroic must have been great. But the scene is framed by Farmer Leo, the crabby know-it-all and a most uncooperative farmer. He's the raw material the promoters have to deal with. Then the acres are signed up through all kinds of comic ruses; the chocolate cake trick, the hair cut, the hem shortening, the guy who locked his clients in the john, and my favorite — "I started singing 'Red River Valley' and by the time I got finished the first verse they all signed." The advantages to

Original cast. Left to right standing: Andras Tahn (Director), Sharon Bakker, Gerry Stoll (General Manager), Linda Tanner (Secretary), Tom Mauss (Stage Manager), Brenda Leadlay, Susan Martin (Assistant to Director); Left to right, seated: Linda Griffiths, Michael Fahey, Bob Bainborough, Catherine Jackson.

Cast on national tour relaxing in Fairview, Alberta. New cast member Peter Meuse replaced Michael Fahey in national tour. Back row, left to right: David Francis, Lubomir Mykytiuk, Skai Leja; Front row: Bill Prokopchuk, Peter Meuse, Sharon Bakker. (Photo by Karin Melberg, Fairview Post).

the meaning and power of the play. The last show on the Saskatchewan tour is over and the backdrop comes down. The cast is in the van talking about what they will do next. "Where are you going?" "To Toronto for a couple of weeks." "I'll spend a day, maybe two, in Saskatoon." "Let's go back to Shaunavon!" "I'm going to Montreal." "We'll see you there at Christmas."

There's a sudden chill as the collective breaks apart, especially since Saskatchewan will mean so little to the largely imported cast: Fahey from the Maritimes, Leja, Francis, Mykytiuk all from Montreal; only Bakker and Prokopchuk are from Saskatchewan. Has it only been another show? It never felt like just another show but something deeper than that. Prokopchuk starts to fiddle. Photographer Barry Perles, with a soundless camera so that people don't know when it's on, keeps his camera running. Over a shoulder we see Sharon Bakker crying, she rubs her eyes, tries to smile. Lubomir Mykytiuk is humming the song, has to hold back tears. Skai Leja smiles her radiant smile at the fiddle player. Stage manager and driver Lynn Hostein smiles back over her shoulder. The bond between the cast is suddenly deep, like we think it was between pioneers of the early cooperators. The moment is poignant. The scene is replaced by another, the main street of a Saskatchewan town in winter, the van driving toward us and the fiddle music dying on the sound track as the voices from the opening scene in the play and film come back. The camera has panned to look at the one-storey false fronts of the town. They look so insubstantial, so fragile. The last line of the opening scene is spoken: "I felt like everything was ahead of me, just waiting for me to meet it."

telling the heroic story that way are two — it is always fun and it is never sentimental.

Paper Wheat does make us laugh and think. It also makes us cry, perhaps even at that funny moment when Farmer Leo joins the Pool because victory has been gained. Though without the laughter and ideas the play would fail, it is still its ability to move an audience deeply that explains its remarkable success. There is a sequence at the end of the Albert Kish film of *Paper Wheat* which is a marvellous extension of

The play shows us intensely things we know well, how people come together to work, how important and substantial human endeavor can be. The way *Paper Wheat* came together and the way it was performed are examples in action of the values the play supports. To make a cooperative is the work of a hundred hands; to make a collective like *Paper Wheat* is also the work of a hundred hands, and of so much skill — even enough to measure up to the skill of the farmer and his wife who proved up that quarter section in the early years and organized the great cooperatives.

Recollections of the Making of Paper Wheat

Recollections of the Making of Paper Wheat

Bob Bainborough

I was in Vancouver when Andy Tahn phoned. I'd been trying to get an acting job on the coast for six months, with no luck. Andy said that 25th Street Theatre was doing a collective play on the cooperative movement and was I interested. Well, I'd never improvised and I didn't have a clue what a cooperative was, but a job, my first acting job, sounded great.

We rehearsed in a church and I remember the pattern on the carpet, but not the name of the church. We talked. It turned out no one was too sure what a cooperative was. Andy said he knew. He was filled with the energy that only Andy can muster. The plan was to go out and interview people who had started or were involved in the cooperative movement on the prairies. We were to bring back stories and characters and do them for the group — simple. O.K. Off we went.

The people we met on these forays to collect stories were amazing. They let us into their homes, fed us tea and cookies and told us their life stories. In Kindersley, Eston, Wakaw, Indian Head, Regina; we were left full of warmth and awe for what they had begun and inspired by their ideals and humanity. The experience was like looking at a mountain. You didn't know whether to laugh or cry or run up it or take pictures of it or just stand and look at it.

As the weeks went by we gathered a lot of experiences, stories and characters. We always met in the Sunday School room of the church and during rehearsals I stared at the carpet a lot — I guess that's why I remember it so well. The idea was to take what we'd seen and heard and make sense of it all. Andy insisted we do scenes and stories based on our discoveries about the pioneers. So we did. For weeks we did pioneer scenes. We had folks go through fires, drought, dust storms, grasshoppers, every other prairie pestilence. We had breaking sod scenes, taking grain to market scenes, having a baby scenes, burying a baby scenes. It must have been quite a sight to see; the entire cast, their eyes shielded from a prairie storm, bent at the waist marching resolutely across that yellow and orange checkered Sunday School carpet, forcing themselves on against all odds in a steady flow to the cloak room. Things got a little melodramatic at times.

With only about a week to go, Andy thought it was time to put the show together. We were supposed to tell the story of the cooperative movement but all our scenes were about early immigrants and pioneers. Oh, oh! A quick rethink. Maybe by concentrating on the grain cooperatives we'll be all right.

We were scheduled to open in Sintaluta, the place where much of the organizational work was done to start fair grain marketing practices. It was also the site of the first grain cooperative in Saskatchewan and was near the original homestead of E. A. Partridge, a great philosopher and organizer in Saskatchewan. I studied E. A. Partridge. I met his sister, I read his book. I researched E. A. Partridge until I dreamed about him. The only thing I didn't want was to play E. A. Partridge in the show — the co-op show that was now the wheat show. The rest of the cast thought this was ridiculous and I ended up playing Mr. Partridge anyway. I don't know why I made such a fuss but I guess I felt he was larger than life and I was over-awed by him.

Our rehearsals moved from the church to Sintaluta the day before opening. We had five or six hours worth of scenes in the show, most of which we'd rehearsed only once or twice. Over the next twenty-four hours we whittled it down. There was a lot of yelling, screaming, and bickering — we were all exhausted and tense.

I remember wishing, a few hours before opening, that someone would just take care of it all and let me know which scenes would be in. Something like that did happen. As the curtain opened for our pemiere, we had a list of the chosen scenes tacked up backstage. We had never run through the entire play . . . yet. This was it.

The community hall in Sintaluta was packed. There must have been 350 people crowded into a hall designed for 150 or so. They sat through three hours of scenes and went crazy at the end. I have never experienced a moment like that curtain call. The hall was cheering and yelling and clapping and standing — all hell had broken loose. It was the most gratifying and exciting moment I have ever experienced. It was indescribable. Was the play that good? No. In fact, it was awful. But there was a spark there that those people in Sintaluta saw and liked.

Paper Wheat
25th Street Theatre

Paper Wheat
25th Street Theatre

Paper Wheat was first produced by the 25th Street House Theatre and was created and performed by Linda Griffiths, Sharon Bakker, Michael Fahey, Bob Bainborough, Brenda Leadley and Catherine Jaxon.

It was conceived and directed by Andras Tahn; design was by Aidan Beck; stage manager was Tom Mauss, assisted by Susan Martin; tour arranged by Gerry Stoll.

Paper Wheat premiered March 18, 1977 in Memorial Hall, Sintaluta, Saskatchewan.

It was remounted by 25th Street Theatre for a thirty-three town Saskatchewan tour in the fall of 1977 with Michael Fahey, Sharon Bakker, Skai Leja, Lubomir Mykytiuk, David Francis and fiddler Bill Prokopchuk under the direction of Guy Sprung. Design was by C. Zak, Stage manager was Lynne Hostein and Richard Rinder was technical director.

A national tour of *Paper Wheat* from June to December, 1979, opened at Theatre Calgary on June 5 with Sharon Bakker, Skai Leja, Lubomir Mykytiuk, David Francis, Peter Meuse and fiddler Bill Prokopchuk. It was again directed by Guy Sprung with design by C. Zak. Stage manager was Allan Meuse; Steve Gregg was technical director and assistant stage manager; costumiere was Kate McDonald.

The company of actors take on roles as required by the play. For example, in one version, Lubomir Mykytiuk played Vasil Havryshyn, Ed Partridge, the Juggler, Mr. Gilanders and various roles in the formation of the Wheat Pool sequence. Sharon Bakker played Elizabeth Postlethwaite, Mrs. Williams, Louie's mother, Farmer Leo and the elevator agent.

Cast of Characters

Vasil Havryshyn	*Ukrainian immigrant*
Sean Phelan	*Irish immigrant*
William Postlethwaite	*English immigrant*
Elizabeth Postlethwaite	*His wife*
Anna Lutz	*Latvian immigrant*
Bill Prokopchuk	*Fiddler*
Ed Partridge	*Sintaluta farmer, first president of Grain Growers' Grain Company*
Louise Lucas	*C.C.F. organizer*
Farmer Leo	*Every Saskatchewan farmer*
John Pearson	*Store owner*
Elevator agent	
Mr. & Mrs. Williams	*Retired farmers today*
Mr. & Mrs. Gilanders	*Retired farmers today*
Louie, Sis, Mom and Dad	*A farming family today*
Old sodbuster	*Retired farmer*

Grain Exchange wheelers and dealers, CBC employees, various men and women as required.

ACT ONE

The last best West

Sean Phelan, Vasil Havryshyn, Anna Lutz, Elizabeth Postlethwaite, William Postlethwaite *and the* Fiddler *are on a train traveling west through the Prairies. The train is approaching as the scene progresses.*

SEAN: I was over in Liverpool looking for work and I was walking down the street this one day, and I saw this sign. It said 'Come to Canada', and in the picture they got these golden fields of flowing wheat. Well, coming from an Irish family of eighteen I thought to myself . . . I'll give it a try.

ALL: (*Sung*)
Roll out, Roll out,
Roll out those rails.
Roll out those rails.
Roll out.
(*Continue refrain during speeches*)

VASIL: I come to Canada alone. In Ukraina I was youngest son. There were eight sons. We were . . . poor. I could not even marry. I hear that in Canada there is land. I tell my father. My father say, "You are young. You go. I'm too old." So I go.

ALL: Roll out, Roll out,
Roll out those rails.
Roll out those rails.
Roll out.

ANNA: We are almost in Winnipeg, on the train from St. Paul, Minnesota, when the conductor comes through the car and tells us we are in Canada now. My younger brother and sister get very excited. They run to the window to see if it looks any different here. But I was just frightened.

ALL: (*Sung*)
We got sixty million dollars' ridin' on this game
We can't let our iron horse pull up lame
Our national dream is a monetary scheme
I said roll out, roll out, roll out those rails,
Roll out those rails,
Roll out.

WILLIAM: Well, I had taken over my father's farm in Lancashire. My brothers all went to work in the mill, the poor sods. It was really mucky in the city. Even over the farm it was getting smokier every year. I was trying to scratch a living out of it, but there wasn't much in it. Most of what I made went to the upper classes. What's more, I had to put up with those nobs chasing their bloody foxes across my land all the time. I heard there was land going cheap in the west of Canada, so I decided I'd come. To be my own master.

ALL: (*Sung*)
Well the Yankees in the south are showin' their aggression
The merchants in the East are having a depression
Got to get the resources from the West to the East
Load 'em all on the Iron Beast.
I said roll out . . . (*etc.*)

ELIZABETH: When I was sitting on the train in Toronto next to my new husband I was so excited . . . I was even more excited than the day we got married. I felt like everything was ahead of me, just waiting for me to get off the train and meet it.

ALL: Well, Louis Riel he was on the rise
With the Indian and the Metis and a battle cry.
We sent troops on the railroad to beat 'em at Batoche
Now ship the immigrants to pay the cost.
I said roll out, roll out, roll out those rails,
Roll out those rails.
Roll out.

(*The* Fiddler *high-balls into the Orange Blossom Special*)

Welcome to Saskatchewan

Vasil *enters with land deed in hand and is met by* John Pearson, *shop owner*

JOHN: Nice day.

VASIL: No speak English.

JOHN: Sprechen zie Deutsch?

VASIL: No.

JOHN: Yak sia mayesh?

VASIL: Shcho? Ti hovorish po Ukrainski? Znayesh, ti pershiy cholovik ya piznav, vid koli ya priyichav do Kanadi, yakiy hovorit po Ukrainski. Nu, yak sya mayesh, yak sya mayesh?

JOHN: Ukrainian, eh? I knew I'd figure it out sooner or later. I speak a little Ukrainian.

VASIL: Oho! Little Ukrainian!

JOHN: English.

VASIL: Oho! English!

JOHN: You got land?

VASIL: Land!

JOHN: Gonna be a farmer, eh?

VASIL: Farming! Farming!

JOHN: Good strong farmer. You need a horse? (Vasil *doesn't understand 'horse'.*) "Kiny?" Do you need a "kiny"?

VASIL: O, ti hovorish pro konya. Tak, tak, meni treba konya bo ya meshkayu tri mili zvitse, i ne tak lehko tam zayichati.

JOHN: Oh ya, you'll need a wagon, too.

VASIL: Aha!

JOHN: I have a store. (Vasil *doesn't comprehend*) "Sklep"

VASIL: O, ti mayesh sklep. Duzhe harno!

JOHN: I have "sklep". You need

Lubomir Mykytiuk and Michael Fahey in "Welcome to Saskatchewan".

"kiny". Come with me. I'll show you around town. Well, so you're new in these parts? Well, here's my store. John Pearson is the name. John Pearson — farmer's friend.

VASIL: Vasil Havryshyn — Havryshyn.

JOHN: Pleased to meet you. Let go of my hand. (*Shouting to back of store*) Charlie! A number two coming up, complete with horse and wagon. Just load it up and bring it around the front. So you need a "kiny"?

VASIL: Tak, tak, bo ya tam shcho dnya budu yichati, i ne tak lechko tam zayichati.

JOHN: Ya!! We'll get you that wagon, too. (*Starts checking off a list*) Let me see, you got a cow?

VASIL: Cow?

JOHN: "Moloko".

VASIL: Moloko? O, ti hovorish pro

39

korovu. To takvo sya robit iz korovoyu. (*Mimes milking cow*)

JOHN: Well, let's see now. You'll need a house.

VASIL: House?

JOHN: House. (*Tries it in Ukrainian*) Chata ... ch ... ch ...

VASIL: O, chato. Tak, tak, ya budu buduvati chatu.

JOHN: Musish mati chatu.

VASIL: Mushu mati. Znayesh, ti cholero, ti dobre hovorish po Ukrainski. De ti sya tak navchiv?

JOHN: Nice talking to you, too. Now, let me see, you'll need lots of food for the winter. Cold winters. Lots of snow. Brrrrrr. Cold. Food.

VASIL: (*Doesn't understand*) ... food?

JOHN: Yisti.

VASIL: Nu pevne, ya lyublyu yisti.

JOHN: We'll give you a hundred pounds of pork, a hundred pounds of flour, and a hundred pounds of prunes. That'll keep you going for the winter.

VASIL: Aha.

JOHN: You just sign right here on the dotted line.

VASIL: How much? I have money.

JOHN: You put your money away. You pay later.

VASIL: I working ... (*Tries to mime "paying after harvest"*)

JOHN: You work. Work hard. Come time of the harvest ...

VASIL: I working ... (*Same attempt at mime*)

JOHN: Come time of the harvest you pay me then. Platy potomo.

VASIL: Ah, platee potomo; dobre. Nu, dobre, ya sya pitpishu.

JOHN: Don't worry about the small print it just says there that if you don't pay me by the harvest I get the implements back ... and all of your land.

VASIL: Nu, dobre, ya sya pitpishu. Vasil — Vasil Havryshyn.

JOHN: (*Leading* Vasil *out the door*) Well, it's a pleasure doing business with you. John Pearson's the name. John Pearson — farmer's friend. Welcome to Saskatchewan. Your horse and wagon are right around the corner. (*Exit* Vasil *to back of store*) Well, Charlie, he looks like he might make a go of it. But don't worry, the odds are in our favor. That's the fifth time we've sold that stuff.

Smells

ANNA: When I got off the train in Swift Current, I stepped down into about seven inches of mud. I was stuck for a time but that is not important. You see it was springtime and that seems to be what happens here. The most important thing that happened to me was I felt like my nose had just exploded. I was breathing in the warm smell of hay and horses that came from the livery stable across the street and the wind from the prairie smells so wet and clean — like rain. And suddenly the whole world smells so fresh and new and I don't mind so much that I still stink like the train. Mamma's English was so bad I left her at the station with the children to look after the luggage while I went into town to look for a place to stay. It was springtime and the streets were so full of mud and puddles and horse droppings. There was wagon wheels that went through the mud and there were horses pulling the wagons and all kinds of men and families on the wagons and they all added their little bit to the smells. There were new buildings going up all over the place. There was the smell of the men sawing wood

40

Linda Griffiths in "Smells" (original production).

Skai Leja in a later production of "Smells".

and the sawdust mixed with the mud that mixed with the horses that mixed with the men and the sun that was beating down on the whole thing. I tell you it was something! It was a wonderful place and that's not even talking about the people. Now the people they came from everywhere. You had peasants and kulaks and bakers, dandies and musicians and men all muscled for work. You walked into a store and there were huge bands of kubasa and beef and chicken hanging from the ceiling. And I don't have to tell you what that smells like. There was the smell of perogies and goulash and all kinds of dough. There were remittance men with their smelly water and handkerchiefs next to English ladies that put Lavender talcum powder on themselves. And right next to them stood Roumanian armpits. Men ready to work and get at it. The whole lot of 'em had been on the boat and train for months. They smelled like something let me tell you. With all those smells in the whole place there'd be that spring prairie wind come down and warm it all together and then it would be a melting pot. People used to say we were a

41

melting pot of people. We were a melting pot of smells! That's right. All swirled together and (*sniffs*) it made you feel alive. All the way home in the dark, momma, I could smell nothing but wood smoke and food cooking, cabbage boiling, meat roasting and fish frying and bread baking. And suddenly I smelled your poutra — Latvian poutra — boiled barley with fried onions and gravy. Oh momma that was the best smell of all!

Squeezing the land

Elizabeth *and* William *tell the story of their land by folding, furrowing and squeezing a rough grey blanket on a table.*

ELIZABETH: We came to this land.

WILLIAM: Our homestead.

ELIZABETH: We cut the bush off it.

WILLIAM: We took up all the rocks.

ELIZABETH: And started breaking the sod.

WILLIAM: We ploughed it all up.

ELIZABETH: Deep furrows in the soil.

WILLIAM: The first year, with the help of some neighbors, we managed to break our full ten acres.

ELIZABETH: And we planted a crop.

WILLIAM: Wheat. It wasn't a bad crop.

ELIZABETH: So we gathered it up and took it to town.

WILLIAM: Well, the price we got for it wasn't quite what we expected.

ELIZABETH: But it was enough to pay the bills and buy some good seed grain.

WILLIAM: So the next year we broke our full quarter and put it all in wheat.

The popular scene "Squeezing the Land" in its original form with actors Bob Bainborough and Sharon Bakker.

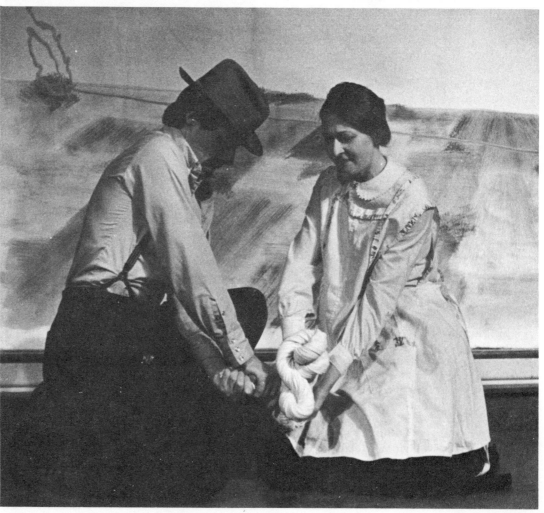

42

ELIZABETH: We got just the right amount of sunshine that year, just the right amount of rain. That wheat grew tall and golden. You should have seen it.

WILLIAM: Aye, we had a bumper crop. We started building the barn and we pre-empted the quarters next to us. Well, then one year . . .

ELIZABETH: The frost hit us early in the fall.

WILLIAM: Well, we got a crop off but it didn't amount to much.

ELIZABETH: The next spring we had to borrow a little money . . .

WILLIAM: We ploughed up around the house . . .

ELIZABETH: Well, all except for the garden patch. We had to have that . . .

WILLIAM: And we were doing all right until the hail came, just about wiped us out.

ELIZABETH: Then, one winter, well, it seemed like it hardly snowed at all, and in the spring it didn't rain. Then the wind started to blow.

WILLIAM: We seeded but the wind blew it all out. It blew off the topsoil, too, up against the house, up against the fence posts, great piles of dust and Russian thistles.

ELIZABETH: It came right through the windows and the cracks in the house. Just a layer of dust all over everything.

WILLIAM: It was the same the next year.

ELIZABETH: And the next.

ELIZABETH and
WILLIAM: (*Together*) And the next.

WILLIAM: We were squeezing everything we could out of that land but it just wouldn't grow anything.

ELIZABETH: It was too dry.

WILLIAM: There's no water left in the well.

ELIZABETH: Nothing will grow anymore. It's too dry. We have to leave here.

WILLIAM: It's my land. I'm not leaving.

ELIZABETH: But it's not worth anything. Nothing will grow here anymore.

WILLIAM: I'm not leaving. There's nowhere else we can go.

ELIZABETH: We have to go. There's nothing left for us here anymore.

WILLIAM: It's my land.

ELIZABETH: Well, look. Just look at your land. It's not worth anything. It's not growing anything anymore.

WILLIAM: We stuck it out somehow.

ELIZABETH: There was no place for us to go.

WILLIAM: We survived.

ELIZABETH: We waited and we hoped.

WILLIAM: Then, one winter, heavy snows came.

ELIZABETH: And in the spring, it rained.

WILLIAM: It rained. All over the fields you could see little green shoots of volunteer wheat! and weeds!

ELIZABETH: I was never so thankful to see weeds in all my life!

WILLIAM: Well, we got a crop in. It wasn't much but it was enough to keep us going. Enough to get us started again.

ELIZABETH: We started treating the land a bit better. We summer fallowed and started rotating the crops.

WILLIAM: And we planted trees for a windbreak, so if a wind like that ever hits us again, we'll be ready for it.

ELIZABETH: We learned how to make a living.

WILLIAM: Aye. This is our living.

ELIZABETH: This is our land.

Prairie wind

COMPANY: The prairie wind is blowing
tonight
The prairie wind is blowing
The prairie wind is a-blowing
tonight
Blowing over my home.

I'm standing alone 'neath the
bright northern lights
My fields are still frozen and
patched brown and white
But the wind on my face has the
feeling of spring
Soon I'll be listening to the
meadow larks sing.

I'll welcome the sweet smelling
wind that brings rain
And the moist smell of earth
giving life to the grain
The fresh breezes rippling the
tender green wheat
And cooling the sweat upon my
back in the summer heat.

But I've known the wind that
blew dry in the Spring
And sucked up the moisture and
parched everything
And piled up the dunes and the
dust by my door
To seep through the cracks and
to creep 'cross the floor.

I've known August winds that
came cold and fast
And hammered the hail on an
anvil of brass
It rattled the windows and
flattened my wheat
In less than an hour I was
battered and beat.

I've fought the wind that carried
the prairie fire's rage
And the sweet scorching smell
of the wheat and the sage
With water, shovels, plows and
sacks we brought it to a stop
But the fire killed a neighbor
and destroyed the crop.

I've cursed when a biting wind
brings on an early frost
When in two wet windy weeks a
bumper crop is lost.
But then the snow sweeps down,
level, white and deep
And the winter wind's whistle
lulls me, as I wait and sleep.

But there are thousands of
winds on the prairie
And each of those winds has its
time,
And the wind isn't always
contrary;
Tonight it is blowing just fine.

Yes, the prairie wind's blowing
softly tonight
The wind's fresh and hopeful
and clear
Oh, prairie wind keep on
blowing just right
And blow me a bountiful year.

The marriage proposal

Anna Lutz *is baking in* Vasil Havryshyn's *kitchen*

VASIL: Good evening, Miss Lutz.

ANNA: Oh, good evening, Mr.
Havryshyn. If you wouldn't
mind, would you please take off
your boots? I just washed the
floor today.

VASIL: Sure. I not know they were
dirty. I take off. Mmmm. You
cook something good.

ANNA: I baked some biscuits for dinner
tonight.

VASIL: Oi! Oi! Oi! I like your biscuits.

ANNA: Aren't you going to take off
your hat?

VASIL: What's wrong with me. Durnă
holorá. I always take hat off
when I eat. Always. Always.
Good. We eat.

ANNA: Could we say grace first, please
if you don't mind?

VASIL: Sure. (*Makes sign of the cross*)
Sure . . . You say.

ANNA: Dear Lord, thank you for the
bountiful meal we are about to
receive. Thank you also for
allowing me to come to work for
Mr. Havryshyn. Amen.

VASIL: Butter?

ANNA: You should have some roast
beef with that, too.

VASIL: Alright. Bozhe miliy, that is
good.

ANNA: I went yesterday to the store and
I noticed there some very nice
material. I thought I could make
some curtains for your windows?
That would make it more
homelike for you.

VASIL: Why we need curtains? We
don't do nothing. Nobody look.

ANNA: I thought since I was here I
could make it more comfortable
for you. But I understand. It's
your house and I don't want to
intrude.

VASIL: How much . . . curtains?

ANNA: Not too much.

VASIL: Alright. You buy.

ANNA: Oh good.

VASIL: Miss Lutz, I want say you
something. You working here
eight months . . .

ANNA: If you are not happy, Mr.
Havryshyn, I can go tomorrow.

VASIL: No, I don't want say that. I
want say you working here
good. You good. You . . .

ANNA: Would you like some coffee?

VASIL: No, thanks.

ANNA: I don't think I want any either.

VASIL: From time you working here, I
know you, you know me.

ANNA: Ya.

VASIL: Well, we get along alright.

ANNA: Ya.

VASIL: We don't argue.

ANNA: No.

VASIL: I thinking to myself. Vasil,
maybe Miss Lutz not working
for you no more. Maybe you
ask Miss Lutz (chort bi to
vzyau) . . . to marry you.

ANNA: Yes.

VASIL: You want get married?

ANNA: Yes. If you want to.

VASIL: Sure. Sure . . . we should marry
soon.

45

ANNA: Yes.

VASIL: Tomorrow? . . . Ah . . . too soon.

ANNA: Yes. Little bit too soon.

VASIL: Sunday?

ANNA: Yes. Sunday would be a very nice day to get married.

VASIL: Sunday. I'm not hungry no more. I go working.

ANNA: I'll keep it warm for you. (*Vasil goes to* Anna)

VASIL: Vasil . . .

ANNA: Anna . . . (*They shake hands*)

VASIL: Anna. Anna. Maybe you get curtains for bedroom window. (*He leaves*)

Michael Fahey in "Consolation".

Consolation

Sean *stands alone in the light.*

SEAN: (*Sung a cappella*)
Well, you know I'm from the Prairies
Where all the wheat is grown
And I'll sing for you a little song
That describes my prairie home.

Well, the land goes on and on and on
And on and on and on
And on and on and on and on
And on and on and on.

And on and on and on and . . .
(*Spoken*) Then there was a tree.

And on and on and on . . .

SEAN: Well, baching on the prairies wasn't exactly the good life without the woman around to take care of the home life. But there was one thing to be said for my tarpaper shack. You could get up in the morning, get washed, make breakfast, have a cup of tea . . . and not even get out of bed.

The broken plow

Elizabeth *is baking bread. Enter* William.

ELIZABETH: Bloody stove! Oh Willy! (*She kicks the oven door shut*) What are you doing in so early? (William *throws his hat on the table*) Something the matter?

WILLIAM: Aye. There is.

ELIZABETH: What's wrong?

WILLIAM: I broke the bloody plow.

ELIZABETH: How did you do that?

WILLIAM: I ran into a bleeding great rock. That's how.

ELIZABETH: Can you fix it?

WILLIAM: No. It's broke clean in two.

ELIZABETH: We've got to get our ten acres plowed. We're already behind, Willie.

WILLIAM: I know we're behind Elizabeth. Look, please don't get at me. It's just one thing after another. It took me two weeks to work out how to hitch the ox and the cow into a team.

ELIZABETH: But we have to do something.

WILLIAM: Well, we'll just have to buy a new blade, I suppose.

ELIZABETH: We've got nothing left to sell.

WILLIAM: Look, give us a cup of tea, will you, love.

VASIL: (*From outdoors*) Hello.

ELIZABETH: There's somebody at the door . . .

WILLIAM: (*Whisper*) We're not home.

ELIZABETH: But the horse is standing right outside. He knows we're home.

VASIL: Hello.

WILLIAM: Well, just don't ask him in.

ELIZABETH: Don't be silly.

VASIL: Hello Mrs. How are you?

ELIZABETH: Won't you come in?

VASIL: Thank you very much (*Enters*). Havryshyn.

WILLIAM: What?

VASIL: Havryshyn. Ukrainian name.

WILLIAM: Postlethwaite. English name.

VASIL: Ah! P . . . Pos . . . Postlethw . . . Very good. Very good.

ELIZABETH: Won't you sit down.

VASIL: Thank you very much.

ELIZABETH: Can I get you some tea?

VASIL: Tea. Very nice, Mrs . . . Mr. Postle . . . Postle . . . ? Ay-yi-yi!

WILLIAM: Postlethwaite.

VASIL: Ah! Ah! Ah! Ah!

WILLIAM: You can call me Bill.

VASIL: Bill. You Bill? I Bill too.

WILLIAM: Bill?

VASIL: In Ukrainian, Vasil. In English, Bill.

WILLIAM: You're joking.

VASIL: No.

WILLIAM: Who would have guessed.

VASIL: Cigarette?

WILLIAM: Oh no. Thanks very much but I've only . . .

VASIL: Oh . . . take!

WILLIAM: Well, ta very much. Here, drink your tea. (*Inhales, chokes*) Excuse me, this is the first cigarette I've had in about . . .

ELIZABETH: Four months.

VASIL: Good. It's a beautiful day.

ELIZABETH: Yes, lovely.

WILLIAM: Aye, it's great.

VASIL: You no working?

WILLIAM: Aye, of course I'm working. I've just come in for a cup of tea.

VASIL: Ah! I finished plow everything. My crop is in. Everything. Finish. Spravasky nchyne.

ELIZABETH: Oh. That's good.

WILLIAM: I suppose that's you down the road, then.

VASIL: Next farm to you.

WILLIAM: Aye, I've passed you by.

VASIL: I see you too. I tell you true Mr. Postle . . . Postle-Bill. I passing by your field. I look. I see your plow and your plow is broken. I think to myself, Vasil, you finish plowing why not go to Mr . . . Bill and offer him your plow.

ELIZABETH: Oh. That's so good of you. You don't know . . .

WILLIAM: Here, hang on Elizabeth. We couldn't do that. It's very kind

47

of you, of course. Mr. Have . . . whatsit . . . but thank you very much anyway. We'll manage.

VASIL: How you manage with no plow?

WILLIAM: We'll manage. We've managed up to now. We'll get by.

VASIL: Ahah! Ahah! You manage. Very good. You not here a long time? Mrs?

ELIZABETH: Since February.

VASIL: February? First winter I was here in Canada, it was hard. I remember, Mr. Bill. Maybe you do me favor.

WILLIAM: Oh, what?

VASIL: Maybe you come working for me. The well on my property no good. Maybe you come help me dig new well.

WILLIAM: How long would it take?

VASIL: Five, six day. One week.

WILLIAM: How much could you pay me?

VASIL: I have no money. So, maybe you come working for me. We dig well and I come working for you. We plow. Use my plow. What you think?

WILLIAM: Well (*Pause*) We'd plow first.

VASIL: Sure. Sure. We plow first. Ha! Ha! Ha! American business, eh? (*They shake hands*)

WILLIAM: Drink your tea.

VASIL: Well, thank you very much, Mrs. but I promise Mrs. Havryshyn I go home. If I don't go home she hit me on the head.

WILLIAM: I'll tell you what, Mr. Havroovnik.

VASIL: Havryshyn.

WILLIAM: Aye; Bill. I'll come with you and I'll get the plow right away.

VASIL: Sure. You come. You come.

WILLIAM: Oh, and Bessie. Have another go at the bread, eh, love.

48

Breaking the prairie
Sean *and his two oxen are out plowing.*

SEAN: Eh! Good morning Paddy. How are you this morning? Eh? You'll have to stick out your tongue, then. Well, it doesn't look too bad. How are you, Shamus? Eh? How are you? Well, it's a fine morning for a bit of plowing, isn't it? And this morning, we are going to plow ourselves a nice straight furrow. Well, just because we've never done it before doesn't mean we can't do it now. It'll be a new experience. Right. Paddy, stop staring at the clouds. I know they're pretty. Shamus, you stop eating all the grass. Now! One. Two. Three. Pull! Paddy, you needn't stare at me as if it's my fault the ground's made of stone. We know whose fault that is but we're not mentioning His name. Alright now, Paddy let's get down to it. You too, Shamus. Alright! Ready. Set. Pull! Look, Paddy, I know you're the leader of this little conspiracy so if you don't hurry up and pull, I'll boot you so hard I'll wrinkle your forehead. Pull! Come on, pull I said. Pull! And I mean pull. Now pull you sons o' churls! Pull! Pull! You, Protestants you! (*The oxen gallop off*) Paddy, you're not a Protestant, you're not a Protestant! Alright! (*He has caught up to the oxen again*). Now, look what you did. You didn't even make a scratch, you didn't even tickle the grass. Alright. Alright. I don't mind if we take a bit of a rest. Oh, but it's fun breaking the prairie. I'll write a poem about it, and send it back to Ireland. They'll love it there. Alright, Paddy and Shamus. Look, I'll be changing your names to Lean and Hungry pretty damn quick. Alright. Alright. Come on, I'll make a deal with the two of you. Alright? If things go bad again this year, if the prices go down and that little worm of an elevator agent cheats us just one more time, we'll go back in the boat to Ireland, the three of us. I'll buy you a round of Guinness. (*The oxen start*

plowing) That's the spirit! That's it! I love the two of you. Aye, you're wonderful beasts. No, no, no, Paddy, not that way! No! No! Paddy! Why you Protestant! You . . . (Sean *is dragged off by the oxen*)

Homesick blues

WILLIAM: (*Spoken*)
It's the closeness of people back there. Back home, people were so close. Well, I could sit in my own kitchen and spit on my neighbor. There's nothing like it here.
(*Sung*)
I wish I were in Liverpool,
Liverpool town where I was born
There are no trees, no humming bees
Nor fields of waving corn.

ELIZABETH: (*Spoken*)
It's hard to get a home started out here. I'm glad we brought Mother's chairs with us.
(*Sung*)
If you should pass my home,
My most beloved home.

VASIL: (*Spoken*)
You know Bill, in my village still in Ukraina, we had a little lake. When I was small boy, I

played there so many times. I used to sing song about boat on the water and the moon shining.
(*Sung*)
Choven chitayetsya sered vodi
Plesche o chvili veslo
Misyats siyaye, biliyuts sadi
Z daleka viduo selo

SEAN: (*Spoken*)
You know what these Prairies need. Well, it's a few more Irishmen around. Maybe then, everything would be a bit greener.
(*Sung*)
So fare thee well, sweet Donegal
The Rosses and Gweedore
I'm crossing the main ocean
Where stormy billows roll.

ANNA: (*Spoken*)
In Latvia, at this time of year, the apple trees are in bloom, and the lilacs. We have planted trees, but it will be years before we see apples.
(*Sung*)
(*Any traditional Latvian song. All join humming. Followed by a fiddle tune.*)

SEAN: (*Spoken*)
Well, you know I went back to Ireland, but it just wasn't the same. So I jumped on the boat and I came home. I guess I missed me mice and me tarpaper shack.

49

Old Bessie

Elizabeth is sorting through her washing, cooking lunch, and ironing.

WILLIAM: (*Enters smoking a cigarette*) Hello, love.

ELIZABETH: Hello, Willie.

WILLIAM: It's a scorcher, today.

ELIZABETH: Yes. It's hot!

WILLIAM: Is lunch ready yet?

ELIZABETH: Lunch! I haven't even finished the breakfast dishes yet. I'm sorry. Willie, I was out doing the wash.

WILLIAM: Oh, it's alright, love. I can wait

Bob Bainborough as Sean Phelan in the original production of "Old Bessie". Bob created this scene for the premiere in Sintaluta. It also appeared in the national production which toured across Canada.

50

a minute. Well, I've got a load of grain ready to take into town tomorrow . . .

ELIZABETH: Oh . . .

WILLIAM: And I might go to that meeting tomorrow.

ELIZABETH: Good.

WILLIAM: So I'll need a clean shirt. Alright?

ELIZABETH: Well, I've got one right here. I'll just press it up for you.

WILLIAM: I think there's a button missing off that one.

ELIZABETH: Well I wonder where that got to. I'll find one and put it back on.

WILLIAM: I'll be up early so you'll have to milk the cow. Alright?

ELIZABETH: Oh alright. I like milking the cow.

WILLIAM: And you'd best give the chicken coop a clean out too.

ELIZABETH: What time do you have to get up?

WILLIAM: About three, I think.

ELIZABETH: Alright. I'll wake you up, make you breakfast, and pack you a nice lunch so you don't have to eat at the hotel.

WILLIAM: There's something else that needs doing here tomorrow. Do you remember what it was?

ELIZABETH: The garden fence needs fixing. The calf keeps getting in.

WILLIAM: Aye; well you'll find the gloves and the shears in the shed, love. And put the gloves on this time, eh. You don't want to be cutting yourself again.

ELIZABETH: Yes, Willie.

WILLIAM: You'd better put some more poison down for the gophers, too.

ELIZABETH: The potatoes. They should come out, don't you think.

"Old Bessie" as it appeared in the provincial tour. Sharon Bakker stands in the background working while David Francis, Michael Fahey (guitar) and Bill Prokopchuk (fiddle) join in a melody.

WILLIAM: Aye, you'd best do that tomorrow. How's lunch doing?

ELIZABETH: Well, it's not ready, yet. I'd like to clean up a bit here, if you don't mind. I'm really sorry, Willie, but I got a bit behind this morning.

WILLIAM: That's alright. I'll tell you what. While you're getting it ready I'll go and have a sit-down on the porch. I'm a bit tired. (*He goes and sits on the porch*)

SEAN: (*Enters*) Hello Bill!

WILLIAM: Hello, Sean, how are you?

SEAN: Good. How are things?

WILLIAM: Oh, busy. Busy!

SEAN: Not too busy for a song, I hope.

WILLIAM: Oh no. Lunch isn't ready yet. (Fiddler *enters*) Oh hello, Bill, how are you doing? You're just in time for a tune.

SEAN: Strike her up.

(*While they sing* Elizabeth *continues working at a frenzied pace in the kitchen*)

SEAN and
WILLIAM: (*Sung*)
I drove a Massey Ferguson; I've

run with the old John Deere,
But nothing ever did the work like the Bessie I hold dear.
She can pull a plow or milk a cow, wash laundry on the board,
Bend her back at the old woodpile until she's cut a cord.

(*Chorus*)
Oh, Bessie, someday you'll be heaven bound,
You'll go to meet your maker, you'll be six feet underground.
But Bessie, until the day when you're set free.
Get up old girl, and do your chores, you're workin' free for me.

I've seen her haul a rack of hay that'd break a camel's back,
She bore me fifteen children in our little sod house shack,
She's hauled our grain in the dead of night, pulled the horses from the mire,
One night she nursed me through the flu and fought a prairie fire.

(*Chorus*)

You can talk about your tractors 'til you're blue in the face,
I wouldn't trade old Bessie for a

51

hundred horse power Case.
Oh, I seen better lookers with
their hair all piled in tiers,
But Bessie, she's a worker; we've
been married fifty years.

(*Chorus*)

(Elizabeth *comes out and ties an apron on*
William)

His grain is just a bit better than everyone else's

ELIZABETH: (*Feeding the chickens*) Here, chick, chick, chick, chick. Here, chick. Here, chick, chick, chick. There you go. Now. Ah, you don't mind that I'm trying to fatten you up for winter, do

you? Winter . . . somebody's coming over there. Oh, I wish Bill were home. Maybe it's someone coming to do us some mischief. Maybe it's somebody coming to steal the chickens. Ah, who'd be walking all the way out here to steal a bunch of skinny little hens? (*To the chickens*) Oh, I'm sorry. Oh, it's a woman. (*Runs into house, straightens it up and fixes her hair. Goes out on porch*)

ELIZABETH: Mrs. Havryshyn?

ANNA: Ya. You must be Mrs. Postlethwaite.

ELIZABETH: Elizabeth.

ANNA: Anna.

ELIZABETH: I've heard so much about you from your husband when he was over here with the plough.

ANNA: Oh, ya.

ELIZABETH: Good to meet you finally. Come in.

ANNA: You're sure you're not busy. I am not disturbing you.

ELIZABETH: Not at all. Come in, come in.

ANNA: Oh, you have a very nice house.

ELIZABETH: Oh, it's not much.

ANNA: But very cozy.

ELIZABETH: It's hard to keep clean at times.

ANNA: Oh, I know how the men track in dirt.

ELIZABETH: Please sit down.

ANNA: Oh, thank you.

ELIZABETH: Will you share some tea with me?

ANNA: Ya. Thank you. You're so now. You're not in the middle of something else.

ELIZABETH: No. No. I'm not doing anything.

ANNA: I see you working. You seem so busy, I don't know whether I should disturb you or not.

ELIZABETH: Don't let that bother you. Just come over anytime.

ANNA: Oh, ya. Mine, too. You know, to tell the truth. I have been thinking about coming for a long time. But always, there seems to be so much work to do.

ELIZABETH: I know what you mean.

ANNA: Today I was pickling beets, right from the morning early. It got so that I think that if I see one more beet or sweep that floor one more time and watch that dust come right back in again . . . I say to myself, you go for a walk. Let the wind clear your head. Maybe see if Mrs. Postlethwaite is home.

ELIZBETH: I'm glad you did, with Bill away . . .

ANNA: Oh, I know. Somedays, I get so alone, I find I'm talking to the pigs. To tell the truth, I would be quite happy not to be at home, tonight when my husband gets back. These days he is always so angry at the price of grain.

ELIZABETH: Willie's so jumpy, somedays I can't even talk to him.

ANNA: You know last week he came home with five dollars for a whole wagon load. Hundred bushels and more.

ELIZABETH: Well, we got the same thing.

ANNA: I tell you that is not enough.

ELIZABETH: We can't live on that! Willie says it's the elevator agent. He's doing it to everybody around here. Did you hear about that meeting tonight? The territorial grain growers' meeting?

ANNA: Ya. My husband read me the notice. I say good. Now you no more yell at me. You go yell where it do some good. He say he don't want to join no organization. I say you don't have to join. Go and talk. Talking don't cost you nothing. Find out why we're getting such bad prices.

ELIZABETH: And we're not the only ones. Somebody somewhere must be doing something about it.

ANNA: Ya. I tell my husband, you get a car from the CPR. Load it up and ship it away. No more of this four and five cents a bushel.

ELIZABETH: Willie says he can't get a car, and even if he could he couldn't fill it himself.

ANNA: Well, why don't we get together. Put all our grain together and ship it away. We'd get better prices than we're getting now.

ELIZABETH: Willie says his grain is just a bit better than everyone else's. He's so stuck up sometimes. He wants to be his own master, do everything by himself.

ANNA: Men, they're like children sometimes. It's good to have a woman . . .

ELIZABETH: To talk to.

Toiling in the broiling sun

SEAN: (Sings)
Toiling in the broiling sun boys.
Toiling in the broiling sun.
We work all day and we pray
It'll last 'till the harvest's done.
Oh Lord one time we ask for rain,
And the next time we ask for sun.
It's a constant battle and a constant gamble,
And I think it's never done.
Toiling in the broiling sun boys,
Toiling in the broiling sun.
We work all day and we pray
It'll last 'till the harvest's done.

Who are the scales working for today?

The dock of a grain elevator. Elevator agent is chewing a fat wad of gum. (Sean enters)

AGENT: Well, hullo. Scorcher, ain't it?

SEAN: Yeah, it's hot alright.

53

AGENT: Now, what you got in here today?

SEAN: Well, I got a load of flax.

AGENT: Yeah? Flax? Well, we'll just check her out.

SEAN: It's Number One. (*Takes a sample, brings it over to table*)

AGENT: Oh, well, we'll just see about that. You're in a bit late, this year, ain't ya?

SEAN: Oh no, no. Well, just a little.

AGENT: Got caught by the rain last week, did you?

SEAN: No, I didn't get a drop.

AGENT: It rained powerful amount in town here.

SEAN: Hit the neighbor bad. Missed me by a mile.

AGENT: It came down cats and dogs.

SEAN: Didn't get a drop.

AGENT: Mm-hmmmm. Mm-hmmmm.

SEAN: What's that?

AGENT: You got a bit of dirt in there.

SEAN: No, no. I scrubbed every grain

meself. Must have been a Canada Goose got me on the way in.

AGENT: Oh you Irish are always joking!

SEAN: The scale's working, eh?

AGENT: Oh, yeah. She's working great.

SEAN: Who for?

AGENT: Alright, we got it. You can just jump in here and shovel it out when you're ready. (*Starts to shovel*) You been farming long?

SEAN: Oh, about two years now.

AGENT: Never would have known it. Just sweep it out here. (*Hands Sean a broom*) Wouldn't want to lose any, eh?

SEAN: Heaven forbid! (*Finishes sweeping*)

AGENT: Just put the broom over there, if you don't mind. (*While Sean is distracted, Agent pulls gum out of mouth and sticks on arm of scales. Locks the scale off at new reading. Then removes gum before Sean notices*) Well, we've got her.

SEAN: Well, that was quick. How much she come to then?

AGENT: I'm just figuring it out here.

Looks like you've got fifty bushels of Number Four.

SEAN: What?

AGENT: Fifty bushels of Number Four.

SEAN: Fifty bushels?

AGENT: That's right.

SEAN: But last week when I came in here with the same wagon filled to the same level you told me it was seventy bushels of Number Two. It's the same crop.

AGENT: That was last week. There's your ticket, mister.

SEAN: What the hell has the week got to do with it?

AGENT: Listen, mister. Just take it or leave it.

SEAN: But you've already got me grain in your bloody bin. What the hell am I supposed to do?

AGENT: Well, I'll see you next year, eh?

SEAN: I hope not.

Exercise!

The coffee shop in town. Vasil *enters.*

VASIL: Rose, coffee. (*Throws his hat on the table.* William Postlethwaite *enters*)

WILLIAM: Hello, petal. Coffee.

VASIL: How much, Bill?

WILLIAM: Five cents a bloody bushel.

VASIL: Five cents. Very good, I got four cents.

WILLIAM: Four cents. Bloody hell.

VASIL: (*Swears at length in Ukrainian*)

WILLIAM: Right!

VASIL: What do we do in winter?

WILLIAM: What am I going to do in January?

VASIL: Ya. Your wife is like this. (*Indicates pregnant stomach*)

WILLIAM: Yeah. I know she is.

VASIL: They are brothers those elevator agents.

WILLIAM: Look, Bill, are you going to that meeting tonight?

VASIL: I go. (*Sean enters*)

WILLIAM: Alright. I'll go too. Hello, Sean. What did you get for your flax?

SEAN: Six cents.

VASIL: Six?

WILLIAM: Bloody hell. What grade did he give you?

SEAN: Number Four.

WILLIAM: Number Four! .. Number One flax!

SEAN: (*Pounds table*) You're damn right, it was Number One flax.

VASIL: Sean, you go to the meeting tonight and I do you little favor.

SEAN: Sure, I'll go to the meeting. What's the favor?

VASIL: We go to the elevator agent and we get little bit of exercise.

SEAN: Oh, what kind of exercise? (Vasil *rolls up sleeves*) Well, you're talking about the exercise I'm craving.

VASIL: Ya.

WILLIAM: Well Sean. (*Spits on hands*) I'll tell you what. I'll come along . . . and hold your hat.

SEAN: You're welcome to it.

ALL: (*Wink to audience*) Exercise!

(*Blackout*)

55

ACT TWO

1905. Railway station, Sintaluta, Saskatchewan.
Ed Partridge *with suitcase.*

ED
PARTRIDGE: Well, it looks like the train is going to be late, again. I heard a rumor that the train arrived on schedule once. That was four years ago — 1901. Now, I don't know whether that's true or not. I'm Ed Partridge. I've been farming just near Sintaluta here, you know. It'll be twenty years now. If the train ever comes I'm on my way to Winnipeg. I'm paying a visit to that Grain Exchange they have there. A lot of people right around here are getting hot under the collar. I'll tell you a story. When I first started farming, when they skinned the wheat they removed just the bran. Now when they skin the wheat they skin the farmer right along with it. One thing we'd love to know is just how that Grain Exchange works. We figure the best way to find out is to send someone there. That's why I'm here, you see. We'd also like to know why prices fluctuate so much, and who is responsible. Well, frankly, we don't know. But, as sure as I'm sitting here on this hard railroad bench, I'm going to find out. I think that we farmers are like mushrooms: we're kept in the dark and we're fed manure.

Mind you, it's not going to be easy. No one's going to say, "Come on in, Ed, look around." Well, the train is here. You know, a lot of people, a lot of people think that we're only hayseeds, but I believe that we farmers are going to change the world. You can wish me luck.

The grain exchange rag

COMPANY: (*Sung*)
I got wheat to sell; it's not even mine.
It's made of paper and it's

Left to right: Brenda Leadlay, Sharon Bakker, Catherine Jackson and Linda Griffiths from the scene "The Grain Exchange Rag" (original production).

56

David Francis, Lubomir Mykytiuk, Sharon Bakker, Skai Leja and Lynne Hostein in "The Grain Exchange Rag" (provincial tour).

borrowed on time.
I sell short; he sells high;
We all end up with a big piece
    of pie.

There's five companies trading
    and betting,
Hiking and charging, and
    gorging and getting.
Wheat's the thing; money's the
    game;
But win or lose, it's all the same.

It's split second code maneuvers;
Nine o'clock winners; ten
    o'clock losers.
Let's all play Bump the
    Bumpkin,
Doing the Grain Exchange Rag.

Those old farmers haven't a
    prayer;
Who wants high finance in long
    underwear?
We hold the cards; we know the
    tricks;
You'll never get us, 'cause we
    work in cliques.

(*Spoken*)
You say your name is Partridge.
You've come to look around,
To take back to the farmer
Information you have found.
You see that we are busy,
No time for explanations.
So stand aside, you're holding
    up
Financial operations!

(*Sung*)
It's Free Enterprise, American
    Dream
We'll sell you down the river,
    but we'll never lose steam.
That's the Grain Exchange,
    that's the Grain Exchange,
that's . . .

(*Spoken*)
Idealism is fine, but this is the
    real world of dollars and
    cents, and if a man's going to
    get ahead . . .

(*Sung*)
That's the Grain Exchange
    Raaa . . . ag.

The report

1905. Ed Partridge is addressing a meeting of the Territorial Grain Growers' Association in Sintaluta.

ED
PARTRIDGE: Well, that's how the Grain
    Exchange appeared to me. Mind
    you, it wasn't easy finding
    anything out. If you want to
    know how old a horse is you
    have to know which end to look
    into. I spent a good deal of my
    time in Winnipeg knee-deep in
    horse manure. Yes, Mrs. Parker?
    Yes, that's right, you did. You
    asked me to find out about the
    government grain inspectors at

the Winnipeg Grain Exchange. Thank you for putting me on the right track. Well, the inspectors, now this is as far as I could determine, are doing an honest job. Now Jack, don't get all het up over this. I'm here to tell you what I saw not what you'd like me to see. I did find out something else that will interest you, though. I've told you how the Grain Exchange works — they have a futures market there and they speculate in paper wheat. I found out something else. There are twenty odd companies that deal in grain on the exchange. Five of these companies are so big that they have a monopoly on marketing. They determine how high and how low prices will be. I believe that they are in league to undermine the farmer and exploit us in every way possible. I was doing a little arithmetic on my way back from Winnipeg. You know, if one of us has a thousand bushels of grain, and we go to sell that grain, we've got very little bargaining power — we have to pretty well accept what we're offered. If one of us has ten thousand bushels of grain and we go to sell that grain, we've got that much more bargaining power. Now think of this for a moment. Let's say we had one thousand farmers, and each one had, let's say, five thousand bushels of grain, and they decided to put it all together, and they found a way to put it all together — now that's five million bushels of . . . bargaining power. This whole thing is so simple, it's so blame simple, that we've been stepping right over it all this time. Why don't we form a company, why don't we form a grain company, in which all the shareholders are farmers — those that grow the grain. Why don't we buy a seat on the Winnipeg Grain Exchange, and if there is enough of us it won't cost any one of us too much. And why don't we market our own grain. In this way, any profit that the company makes goes right back to the farmer and not some businessman to support his refined habits. Ottawa supports him because he's big business. You know, there's a lot of decent folks out here in the West, who would never have even heard of Ottawa if it wasn't for all the scandal that goes on down there. That's right. You know, I was hoping someone would say that. On my way over to this meeting, I was hoping someone would say, "Ed, we're farmers. What do we know about grain marketing?" A famous philosopher once said that knowledge is power. Well, I agree with that famous philosopher — knowledge is power. But knowledge can be used in two ways. You can hoard knowledge, keep it to yourself, and use it to exploit those who do not possess it. Or, you can share knowledge, and make this a better world for all of us, all of us, to live in. I believe that. Now, what if those

58

who possess the knowledge are not willing to share it? Well, I believe then, that you have to take it. You get right in the middle, right in the thick, you take your knocks, but you learn as you go along. We really don't have any other choice. Now I suggest that we organize a large meeting at a later date and thrash out the details. This will give us a chance to talk things over, discuss amongst ourselves, and argue and if I know some of you, there will be plenty of that arguing. Right, Jack? But I move that here and now, at this meeting, we accept in principle the idea of a cooperative grain marketing company, in which all the profit goes right back to the farmer. Now is there any of you neighbors that will second that motion . . .? Thank you, Jack. Now, all in favor raise your hands . . . thank you neighbors, thank you.

Grain Growers' Grain Company

Four farmers wander on with small sheaves of wheat in their hands, and sorrowful expressions on their faces. They look at each other and back at their wheat then an idea hits them.

Slowly, one by one, they put their individual sheaves together. Their expressions change as all their wheat becomes one big sheaf. A sign appears from the foot of the stage. It reads:

GRAIN GROWERS' GRAIN COMPANY
1905

Mystery theatre

A not yet invented CBC radio studio in the 1910's. General confusion as the mikes are set up and the actors come in talking about last night's parties and the general bad state of the profession. An assistant floor manager yells "Fifteen seconds to air time!" and deposits a box of sound effects on the table. The wrong sound effects. Panic reigns, improvisation ensues: a washboard for typewriter noise, kazoos, blocks of wood, whatever.

DIRECTOR: *(at separate standing mike, doubling as* Announcer *and* The Whistler*)* Ten seconds . . . quiet in the studio . . . five . . . four . . . three . . . two . . . Quiet! . . . *(silence, with dropped effects and ends of conversations)* . . . Good evening, ladies and gentlemen and welcome once again to . . . Mystery Theatre . . .

WHISTLER: *(approaching footsteps, then whistling)* I am known as The Whistler. I see into dark corners, through the silent shadows and behind the closed doors that

David Francis, Sharon Bakker, Michael Fahey and Skai Leja in the "Grain Growers' Grain Company".

hide the unknown activities of this thriving metropolis: WINNIPEG! I see the evil that lurks within the hearts of men . . . and know their thoughts, even before they do. It was early evening in late December, 1908, and in the lofty offices of a grain elevator company, an elevator tycoon had called a meeting of elevator magnates, (*fade in hubbub of voices*) . . . to discuss a matter of the gravest importance . . . (*hubbub crescendo . . . at peak:*)

MAGNATE 1: All I can say is, P.B., this better be a matter of the gravest importance . . .

WHISTLER: . . . grumbled one elevator magnate . . . (*more hubbub . . .*)

TYCOON: GENTLEMEN! . . .

WHISTLER: . . . thundered the tycoon . . .

TYCOON: . . . This is a matter which threatens our very existence. Support is still growing rapidly for that farmers' organization . . . the Grain Growers' Grain Company (*sound: barnyard*) They're syphoning off all our profits! (*uproar from Magnates, cut short and sharp.*)

WHISTLER: There was consternation among the private entrepreneurs . . .

MAGNATE 1: . . . But, P.B., we've tried everything. First we had the banks stop their credit. Then we almost got them kicked off the Grain Exchange. Then we even forced them to stop their system of dividends.

TYCOON: Even so gentlemen, their share of the market has quadrupled this year. They're handling over two million bushels of the farmers' wheat. (*more uproar, cut same*)

WHISTLER: . . . There was even greater consternation.

MAGNATE 1: Do you have any ideas at all, P.B.?

TYCOON: Yes, I think I do. (*sound: 'the plot thickens'*)

WHISTLER: In the following weeks, a number of letters, ridiculing the Grain Growers' Grain Company (*sound: barnyard*) appeared in the five Winnipeg publications, signed by a mysterious . . . Mr. Observer. (*sound: mysterious*) On a dark night, three weeks later, in the offices of the Grain Growers' Guide . . . (*sound: barnyard. Wrong!*) . . . the farmers' weekly rag, a single lamp was burning. George Chipman, the plucky young editor, was putting the finishing touches on a story that could rock the wheat world . . . (*sound: typewriter, paper ripped from machine*) The young editor sprang from his chair and threw his hat in the air . . .

CHIPMAN: . . . That oughta do it . . .

WHISTLER: . . . he told himself with satisfaction. With his instinct for justice, the perseverence of a good sleuth, and the nose of a bloodhound, he thought he had cracked the identity of the mysterious . . . Mr. Observer (*sound*) . . .

CHIPMAN: . . . I think I've cracked the identity of that Mysterious Mr. Observer (*sound*) . . .

WHISTLER: . . . he beamed . . .

CHIPMAN: Now to call him in . . . (*sound: dialling*) . . .

WHISTLER: . . . he called him in . . . (*sound: door slam, approaching footsteps*)

OBSERVER: Smith's the name. You called me in?

CHIPMAN: I called you in Mr. Smith . . .

WHISTLER: . . . said the editor pleasantly, when his visitor's pipe was going smoothly . . . (*sound: sucking pipe to light it . . .*)

CHIPMAN: . . . because I thought you might like to look over this copy (*sound: rustling paper*) before I publish it. I want to be fair and there may be something . . .

WHISTLER: . . . and indeed there was: . . .

OBSERVER: Holy typewriter ribbon! . . .

60

WHISTLER: ... the Mysterious Mr. Observer (*sound: mysterious*) gulped ...

OBSERVER: (*gulps*) ... this blows my cover completely!

CHIPMAN: Yes, Mysterious Mr. Observer (*sound: mysterious*) ... you are a newspaperman and if this article is published, your career will be finished forever.

OBSERVER: Holy jumping newsprint! Don't publish! I'll stop writing those letters.

WHISTLER: His mind raced to the only thing that mattered now (*sound: cash register's opening ring*) ...

OBSERVER: I hope I can still get my salary from those employers. (*sound: car starting, accelerating, traffic noises, horns, screech of brakes ...*)

WHISTLER: ... Fourteen blocks later — in the penthouse palace of the Elevator Tycoon, a conference was under way ... (*sound: hubbub ...*)

TYCOON: I'm sorry to inform you — Mysterious Mr. Observer (*sound: mysterious*) — that the Winnipeg papers have refused to publish any more of your letters, because the farmers have started to cancel their subscriptions by the hundreds ... (*sound: hubbub*) ... Therefore we have decided that we no longer require your services.

MAGNATE 1: However, we are willing to offer you the generous sum of fifteen hundred dollars (*sound: cash register*) to settle your contract.

WHISTLER: The Mysterious Mr. Observer ... (*sound: mysterious*) ... smiled to himself ... (*Director cues sound effect, wrongly, but elicits a smile into the mike from Mr. O.*) ... and answered pleasantly ...

OBSERVER: ... But gentlemen, my contract has a year and a half to run and it is still worth six thousand dollars ... (*sound: cash*) ... however, as a token of goodwill, I would agree to tear it up for a modest — FIVE THOUSAND DOLLARS? (*sound: cash*) ...

MAGNATES: (*exploding*) Outrageous! outrageous! outrageous! outrageous! OUTRAGEOUS!!

WHISTLER: ... The elevator owners were outraged. They answered, not so pleasantly ...

MAGNATE 1: ... You're talking through your hat, young man.

OBSERVER: Maybe so; but it is a five thousand dollar hat! (*sound: cash*)

TYCOON: We have no intention of paying you such a preposterous sum! You should be grateful for the amount we've offered you!

OBSERVER: Gentlemen. Under contract to you, I've been writing letters to the Winnipeg papers, deliberately trying to undermine the farmers' confidence in the Grain Growers' Grain Company ... (*sound: barnyard*) ... I've been using all my intelligence and imagination to bring the farmers' company to its knees — for your benefit. And if it ever got out that you were involved. ...!

MAGNATES: (*gasping*) ... gasp! ... gasp! ... gasp! ...

WHISTLER: ... The elevator owners were beside themselves, and fit to be tied, but he had them over a barrel ...

OBSERVER: ... We'll just let my contract toddle along then and no hard feelings. (*sound: cash*) ...

WHISTLER: ... The Mysterious Mr. Observer ... (*sound: mysterious*) ... got his money. The elevator owners paid him the five thousand dollars ... (*sound: cash*) ... No more denigrating letters, signed by the Mysterious Mr. Observer (*sound: mysterious*) ... were received by the Winnipeg papers. The efforts of the private grain companies to sway public opinion against — the Grain Growers' Grain Company! ... (*sound: barnyard*) ... were foiled again. And — in a small, (*fade in "God Save the King"*) ... but significant way JUSTICE ...

61

was served . . . (*sound: anthem peaks with last word and finishes. Footsteps come in on last four notes, recede, as whistle theme repeats. Silence.*)

ACTOR 1: (*Now doing commercial*) This programme has been brought to you by IVORY SOUP — 99 and 44 one hundredths percent — purée. . . .

ACTOR 2: . . . And by OX-AND-ALL, the all purpose family soap: . . .

ACTORS: (*in tandem*) OX AND ALL . . . OX AND ALL . . . NNHH NNH NNHHH . . . (*kazoo, off key . . .*)

DIRECTOR: . . . We're a little late folks — so good night, let the Good Lord take a likin' to ya, and don't forget to tune in next week, same time, same station, for the next exciting episode of . . . "The Whistler" . . . (*starts to whistle, cut off by klutz actor dropping sound effect, e.g. a cymbal . . . silence regained, director finishes whistle theme. Actors leave in hubbub of conversation; "Deedee, do you want a drink in the upstairs bar?" "Sure." "Four o'clock? . . ."*)

Ed's book

1920's. Ed Partridge is at work at home.

ED
PARTRIDGE: Yes? — (*Looks up at audience from his desk*) Excuse me. I was in the middle of a sentence when you dropped in. (*Finishes writing*) There. Well, it's been some time. I guess you could say a lot has happened. We formed that company, you know, the Grain Growers' Grain Company. I was proud of that. I was president for about a year. Then I decided to step down for a younger man, Mr. Crerar, you might have heard of him. He's done a fine job . . . I'm told. I was a little too forthright in my views for that position. I'm not exactly a diplomat, not exactly a businessman. I'm what you might call an idea man, although some of my ideas don't

sit too well with people, either. But, you know, you can't force-feed people. People will learn at their own pace. I've found that out. Well, I'm writing a book now, and I'm putting it all down. "I am part of all that I have met." My book will talk about what I think is wrong and how to change it. It will talk about Coalsamao, my separate Cooperative Western State, where the land belongs to the people, and I hope it will bear some fruit, somewhere . . . God willing. I just started the book. I am just writing the preface, but I would like to read you part of it to give you some idea of why I'm writing it, and what it's all about. It will say in my book, it's called *War on Povery*, by the way, "There are about three millions of us here, in the West — half of whom are adults — the greater number, though rarely willful idlers, are poor as snakes, often with not as much stake in the country as a badger — that at least has a rent-free hole to live in — and these, for the most part, hopeless as Hell of ever being otherwise. I shall expect this bookish or ghostly conference" — I like to think of my book as a conference — "to be followed by many real, lively, flesh-and-blood gatherings to discover how best and quickest to enlist, oranize, officer, train, equip, and put in the field 'An Army Of The Common Good' to wage a successful, bloodless, life-giving, not life-taking" — I lost two sons in that great war — "wealth-creating, not wealth-destroying, love-and-hope-inspiring, not hate-and-fear-engendering War On Poverty — physical, mental and spiritual. Such is my vision — and mock it not; for 'Where there is no vision the people perish' as we do here." (*Wipes eyes*) Excuse me. The Grain Growers' Grain Company started a newspaper in 1908, it was called the *Grain Growers' Guide*, and I was editor of that . . . for one issue. You see, I had this bonehead idea that it should be read by the working people in the cities and towns as well as by the farmers. But they said I was going too far too fast, "Ed," they said "you can't alter human nature." You can't alter human nature. You know, one thing I like is poetry. There will be quite a bit of poetry in my book. I'd like to read you a bit. It's not very long. It's by a woman. Her name is Charlotte Gilman. It's all about human nature. It goes like this:

"There once was a Neolithic
     Man,
An enterprising wight,
Who made his chopping
     implements
Unusually bright.
Unusually clever he,
Unusually brave,
And he drew delightful
     Mammoths
On the borders of his cave.
To his Neolithic neighbours,
Who were startled and
     surprised,
Said he, "My friends, in course
     of time
We shall be civilized!
We are going to live in cities!
We are going to fight in wars!
We are going to eat three times
     a day
Without a natural cause!
We are going to turn life upside
     down
About a thing called gold!
We are going to want the earth
     and take

As much as we can hold!
We are going to wear great piles
     of stuff
Outside our proper skins!
We are going to have diseases!
And accomplishments!! and
     sins!!
Then they all rose up in fury
Against their boastful friend,
For prehistoric patience
Cometh quickly to an end.
Said one "This is chimerical,

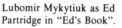
Lubomir Mykytiuk as Ed Partridge in "Ed's Book".

Chorus in backgroud with Lubomir Mykytiuk as Ed Partridge (foreground).

63

Utopian! absurd!"
Said another, "What a stupid life!
Too dull, upon my word!"
Cried all, "Before such things can come,
You idiotic child,
You must alter human nature!"
And they all sat back and smiled.
Thought they 'An answer to that last
It will be hard to find!'
It was a clinching argument
To the Neolithic Mind!"

You know, lately I've been hearing a lot of talk about something people are calling a wheat pool. Now it's a sort of a grain pool; you see now, the idea is to get enough farmers together to actually be able to control the prices and market. And, well, though my energies have found a new home here among these books and papers, I wish them luck. I just hope that they too don't become just another company. But I believe that ideas never die, they change form. You know I've been called all sorts of things in the course of my life — some of which are true — but lately people have taken to calling me the worst thing imaginable. Now I don't want to shock any of you good people — but lately people have taken to calling me — a dreamer. Well, if you'll excuse me, I've got just a little more work. . . .

The man from Sintaluta

COMPANY: (Sung)
There was a man from Sintaluta;
He had a vision within his heart.
He took the stand for the common people,
Against the power that was tearing them apart.
He said,
"What are you worried for?
The worst they can do is kill you.

And if you believe in Heaven, well;
There is nothing to worry about at all."
Try to look from another point of view;
Let's all try to give and take.
If we work together we'll achieve much more.
So now is the time for us to cooperate.
Cooperative Commonwealth,
People working for their own survival.
We don't own the land, we only farm it.
Production for use not profit for the few.
"What are you worried for?
The worst they can do is kill you.
And if you believe in Heaven, well;
There is nothing to worry about at all,
There is nothing to worry about at all."

Leo

1924. Farmer Leo is reading a newspaper on his porch. The Fiddler ties the following scenes together with a reel.

FARMER
LEO: Hello there. I'm a farmer. I farm a fair piece of land around here. Put a couple hundred acres in wheat this year. Though only the Lord knows if I am going to get any money out of it. You know some of my neighbors are backing those farmer organizations. They're pushing for everybody pooling their grain together and selling it cooperatively. Getting back patronage dividends or whatever the hell they call it. Well, they've asked that California lawyer guy back again. You know him. Just a minute. (*shuffles through paper*) Yah, here it is — Aaron Sapiro. They've asked him to come around making speeches again. Well, you know what they are trying to do? They're trying to get fifty per cent of the seeded acreage in all of Saskatchewan signed up for that pool idea. They tried it last year, 1923, but they couldn't make it. So they're

64

taking another stab at it this year. Well, altogether that's six-six-six-mil-million acres they're trying to sign up. Well, they'll never do that!

(The following scenes cut into Farmer Leo's *speeches)*

WOMAN: Well, I baked you a nice chocolate cake. You like chocolate, don't you?

MAN: Yaa.

WOMAN: Look at that icing — mmm good.

MAN: Yaa.

WOMAN: I'll just cut you a nice big piece. You're a growing boy, aren't you?

MAN: Yaa.

WOMAN: And I'll pour some of this thick heavy cream on the top.

MAN: Ooooooo.

WOMAN: Before you begin, I wonder if you would mind signing your John Henry to the Wheat Pool.

MAN: *(Looks at list, looks at* Woman, *looks at cake)* Yaa.

FARMER LEO: They're bragging that they got 6,000 acres signed up the first afternoon. But believe you me. They'll never get any more.

SEAMSTRESS: Stand still Nancy, and don't step on my fingers.

WOMAN: But goodness gracious, what are you doing?

Michael Fahey (standing on chair) as Aaron Sapiro organizing farmers in the scene entitled "Co-op Quickies". It was later incorporated into the "Leo" scene of the revised play.

Sharon Bakker in "Leo".

SEAMSTRESS: I'm raising the hem of your skirt.

WOMAN: But heavens to Betsy, Gertrude, why?

SEAMSTRESS: We promised the men that for every 3,000 we got signed up for the Wheat Pool we'd raise our skirts a quarter of an inch.

WOMAN: But what if they sign up 50,000 names?

SEAMSTRESS: Then you'll have to scrub your knees.

FARMER LEO: 'Prairie Farmers Sign Up Sixty Thousand Acres For Their Wheat Pool' — Hmmm. Still a ways to go to six million, eh?

BARBER: Well, what can I do you for?

CUSTOMER: Can you trim a little off the back, please?

BARBER: Well that depends on what kind of a cut you want.

CUSTOMER: What kind of a cut do you have?

BARBER: Well, there's the Liberal Cut, the Conservative Cut and the Pool Cut.

CUSTOMER: Frankly, I don't know the difference.

BARBER: Well I'll tell you. The Liberal Cut is a nice cut, but I don't think you can afford that one. The Conservative Cut — now that's a nice cut, but you don't want that one either. You come in for a trim and we shave you bald. And then there's the Pool Cut.

CUSTOMER: Pool Cut?

BARBER: Pool Cut . . . now that's a nice cut. We trim your hair just right and we save it. Then when you need it most, we return it to you as a rebate in the form of a wig.

CUSTOMER: Well, I'll take that one.

BARBER: Sign here.

FARMER LEO: It says here they got 60,000 acres signed up so far. Took 'em a while. You know this whole thing reminds me of an old gray mare I used to have, steady but slow . . . too slow. They'll never do it!

(The fiddle begins to get louder)

FARMER 1: I signed up 200,000 acres. I talked and talked and talked and talked and talked and talked. I wouldn't go to bed until they signed.

FARMER 2: I got 1,000 names. That's 250,000 acres. I locked them in the john until they signed.

66

WOMAN: I got the church assembly to sign up over 120,000 acres. I started singing Red River Valley and by the time I got finished the first verse they all signed.

FARMER 3: Our parish priest went out on a marathon sermonizing tour and he signed up 150,000 acres. Yahoo!

FARMER 4: The local branch of the Saskatchewan Grain Growers' Association has rallied their support and signed up 700,000 acres. Yahoo!

GIRL: He's the only boyfriend I've ever had but I know you like him a whole bunch, so if you get your dad to sign up for the Wheat Pool, you can have him. He's already signed? Well, then get your own boyfriend!

FARMER
LEO: Dag-nab-it! It says in here that the Wheat Pool has signed up ... five million ... nine hundred ... ninety-nine thousand eight hundred acres. Well, that means they're about 200 acres short. I've got 200 acres. If I sign up then they'd have six million acres — fifty percent pool. I TOLD YOU WE COULD DO IT!

(*Fiddle goes wild*)

Man enters. Starts to tap, then realizes he has only one shoe on. Girl enters — same thing but missing shoe on opposite foot to man's. Idea strikes. If they tap together, the alternate shoes will make it sound as if one person was tapping. The dance goes from slow and tentative to frenzied ending with the old-fashioned theatrical tam-ta-ta-tam-tam ... tam-tam. They finally turn their backs to the audience, and their two T-shirts together make up the following message:

    WH EAT
    PO OL
    19 24

Wheat Pool song

COMPANY: (*Sung*)
Since the time of Joseph back in Egypt,
Right on down to today,
Someone else has taken all the

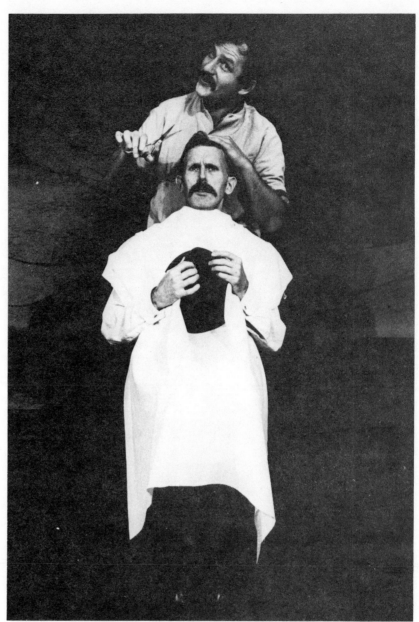

Lubomir Mykytiuk as the barber with David Francis in the chair from the Farmer Leo sequence.

cream of the farm
And left us the milk and whey.
With a little real cooperation
We can help each other along.
Then all over the land on every hand,
We will shout and sing this song:

(*Chorus*)
From the North, South, East, West
All o'er the prairie
Keep the Wheat Pool rolling along.
Tell everybody when you sign your name,
Then ask your neighbor and he'll do the same.
If we all stick together,
What we have we'll hold;
You'll be proud to be a farmer

Back row, left to right: Michael Fahey, Lubomir Mykytiuk, Bill Prokopchuk; Front row, left to right: David Francis, Lynne Hostein, Skai Leja, Sharon Bakker.

Skai Leja as Louise Lucas.

When the story's told.
From the North, South, East, West,
All o'er the prairie
Keep the Wheat Pool rolling along.

Farmer Jones made $20,000 speculating in wheat.
Then the market dropped and he lost all that he had, and he came home badly beat.
Had to buy some seed but had no money. His neighbor said

don't ever fear.
I'll divide up with you, I've enough for two from my Wheat Pool cheque this year.

(*Chorus: From the North, South, etc.*)

Drought

FARMER: After four years of drought, my son had never seen a single drop of rain. One day when he was playing outside, a drop of rain landed right in front of him. Well, he looked at it for awhile, then he looked up to see where it came from and two more hit him on the forehead. Well, he fainted out flat right there on the spot. I had to stoop down, pick up a handful of dirt and throw it on his face. That revived him.

Louise Lucas

(*1930's. A small gathering to celebrate the opening of a cooperative coal shed in Northern Saskatchewan.*)

EMCEE: We have a very special speaker for our opening tonight. Let's give a warm welcome to Mrs. Louise Lucas.

LOUISE: I know at official functions such as this one, it is customary to have one of the local dignitaries speak. Well, I'm not a politician. I'm a farm wife and mother like most of the women here tonight. I'm here to speak about something that distresses me greatly. That is the poverty that exists today in Saskatchewan and throughout Canada. As I was arriving, I passed by the garden in front of your Fire Hall. I cried to see that lovely vegetable patch, those lovely peas and beans and rows of potatoes. In southern Saskatchewan, try though we may, most of us haven't had a garden in four years. A small crop of wheat is about all we can raise. But when we try to sell that wheat, the price we are getting is so low that we can't buy shoes to send our children to school. So now shoe factories

Weyburn Fair, 1927.

WHEAT POOL REST TENT

are closing down or running short-time, and the unemployed factory workers can't afford to buy the milk and butter and eggs and meat that some of us, where there is still water, can produce. Why is it that when harvests are as bad as they have been, that brokers in the grain exchange of Winnipeg and Chicago are still talking about the glut of wheat on the markets of the world, and the price of wheat keeps going down. When we know that in our own province and throughout the world, children are going to bed hungry. We are caught in an economic system that puts human greed above the supplying of human need. The men in control today have lost sight of the means of more evenly distributing the wealth of this country because they are not interested in supplying human need. Their concern is profits — first, last and always. Now does this make sense? Do you not think it is time we put our brains to work to help ourselves? People say to me, "Louise Lucas — you're a Communist!" If you want to call me a Communist because I believe in oranges for the little ones on the farms, and milk for the babies in town, because I believe in humanity first, then

you go right ahead. But I believe that we do not have to suffer this un-Christian waste and inhumanity. I believe we can do something about our economic system to improve our lives and the lives of our children. From the earliest homesteading days the prairie has taught us how to survive by cooperating. When there was a prairie fire, people would come from miles around to help save each other's farms. And when a neighbor needed help to put up a barn, the whole community would help him build it. And when the price of wheat got so low that it was hardly worth the effort to sell it, we got together and created the Wheat Pool. And the Pool has proved that by selling our grain together we can get better prices than we ever could by selling separately. Can you imagine where the price of wheat would be today if it weren't for the Pool? But marketing is not the only area where cooperation works. Your coal shed, the opening of which we are celebrating today is proof that cooperative buying works. And coal is not the only commodity you have been buying this way. Many of you have been sharing bulk lots of gasoline, binder twine and sacks for years now. What's more the

69

oil refinery in Regina is proof that cooperative production is feasible. In one year they made back their original investment and are now expanding. So let's not stop here. Let's include all the things we need for daily life in a program of cooperative buying — food, clothing, building supplies, and household furnishings. Let's have more cooperative enterprises, such as farm implement manufacturers co-op. And why not cooperative health care, and our own money co-ops. Right now we are at the mercy of financial institutions that don't have our interests at heart. So why not pool together our savings in our own credit unions so that we can have access to that money when we need it, without paying crippling interest rates and so that we can control how that money is used.

Why do we only learn from calamity? Why does it take an economic depression of this magnitude, which brings us to the brink of destitution and despair, before we start to implement our cooperative ideas more fully. Why do we have to wait till we see the soil eroding before our eyes from drought and wind before we start to build wind-breaks? Let us build wind-breaks before, not after, the necessity for them occurs. Let cooperation be our windbreak against the future. So that our children will never have to suffer as we are suffering now.

(*1960's rock group bangs straight into Cooperation*)

Co-op song

COMPANY: (*Sings and dances*)
Cooperation, what's it all about?
There ain't no reason to jump and shout.
I want some money and a hot rod car.
Forget the northern lights and prairie stars,
I want to get on the highway and feel the wheels move.
Sell this land and get in the groove.

(*Chorus*)
Cooperation, shoo-bee-do-ah
Cooperation, shoo-bee-do-ah
Cooperation, shoo-bee-do-ah
Cooperation, Cooperation,
Just ain't part of my operation

Saskatchewan is really getting to me,
Take me Big City, I wanna be free.
Gimme, gimme, gimme lots of Free Enterprise.
I've had it up to here with socialist lies.
Now don't tell me I'm trying too hard.
The only pool I want is in my backyard.

(*Chorus*)
Cooperation, shoo-bee-do-ah,
Cooperation, shoo-bee-do-ah,
Cooperation, shoo-bee-do-ah,
Cooperation, Cooperation
Just ain't part of my operation.

Co-op Song. From left: David Francis, Sharon Bakker and Lubomir Mykytiuk.

Togetherness

1970's. Mother, Father and Son gather for the evening meal.

MA: All right, Louie. Come and sit at the supper table now, dear.

LOUIE: (*reading comic book throughout scene*) Yeah, yeah, yeah. I'm coming, Ma . . . hey, what's for supper, Ma?

MA: The usual.

LOUIE: Aw, Ma.

MA: FREEEEED! SUPPER'S READYYY!

PA: I'm coming.

MA: Where's your sister? She's late for supper again!

LOUIE: Hey, how do I know where she is?

MA: Pass the co-op butter, Fred. (Pa *reads newspaper*) Have some co-op milk Louie.

LOUIE: Ma, gee . . .

MA: Pass the co-op pickles, Fred.

PA: Wait just a co-op minute.

MA: Are we going to Arizona again this winter, dear?

PA: No, dear, we can't afford it.

MA: Oh. Well last winter Fred and I decided to take a little holiday. We drove down to Arizona. We met a lot of our neighbors down there. It was a bit like old home week — in Phoenix. Well, before we left, we decided to surprise Sonny here with a new car. And a lot of his buddies had CB radios. So we gave in and got him one of those, too. When we got back we found out he'd traded that radio in on a new one. And then he'd traded that one in on an even bigger model. And he'd rolled the car. The little stinker.

SIS: (*entering*) Hi, Ma. (*hellos*)

PA: Here she comes. Prissy Little Miss Co-op.

SIS: Dad!

MA: Why are you late for supper tonight, dear?

SIS: I told you, ma. I was at the Land-use Policy Meeting.

MA: Was that today?

Louie the Juggler played by Lubomir Mykytiuk with Lynne Hostein as Sis in "Togetherness".

71

PA: Oh-oh. Get your co-op earplugs ready.

SIS: Do you know, there are only half as many farms in Saskatchewan as there were twenty-five years ago? Well, if we don't start fighting back, in another twenty-five years this whole province is going to be nothing but one big foreign-owned corporate farm. You know, Louie, if you wanted to take over Dad's farm now, you couldn't afford to do it.

LOUIE: So who cares. I'm gonna play baseball.

PA: Hockey; I told you, hockey.

LOUIE: Baseball.

MA: Now the co-ops are there to protect us against that kind of thing.

SIS: Ma, co-ops today are a multi-million-dollar operation; they're no different from any other big business. Well, look at the way they treat their employees. Do you know that the employees of at least ten co-ops and credit unions are out on strike in order to get decent wages and better working conditions.

MA: Co-ops are for people — not for employees. Now have some co-op peas dear.

SIS: Yecch. There's nothing co-op about those peas. Those are Libby's rejects with a co-op label slapped on them.

MA: Federated Co-ops wouldn't do a thing like that.

SIS: Oh, Ma, you're so naive.

MA: Oh, look what I got down at the store today, dear. They had a few left over. Federated Co-operatives celebrated their 50th Anniversary last year. Federated is made up of hundreds and hundreds of co-ops all over the country. And we all celebrated. Handed out these souvenir pens. You see, it says right here: "1928 to 1978 — Co-operative Retailing Systems — 100% Canadian made — Made in the U.S.A." — oh. Pass the co-op bread, Fred.

PA: You know some people would drag their ass across forty acres of broken glass to go down to the co-op store to buy a can of co-op peas. Around here when they talk about mixed farming they mean curling and co-ops. Well, the co-ops give me a pain right in the you-know-where. My brother-in-law used to have a funeral home here in town. Until some of the old folk got together and started their own Co-op Funeral Home. Drove him right out of business. Well, I've had the co-ops right up to here. And do you know what N.D.P. stands for? hmm? do you? Naturally Displeased People. Pass the co-op peas.

MA: Have some ham, Fred.

PA: You know, I think I'm going to take my grain down to that new private grain company down the road.

MA & SIS: You are! Oh, Fred, do you think so?

PA: Well, what did you learn in school today, son?

LOUIE: Nothing. But I'll tell your what I didn't learn in school though: all about the price of bread.

MA & PA: Well, why don't you tell us about it.

LOUIE: Ladies and gentlemen — come on, Sis — my mom and my dad have asked my very able assistant — (Sis *gets up with basket of props*) — and I to give you a small, but I hope ample demonstration on how a fragment of our economic system functions. Now the purpose of this demonstration is to show you, the consumer, how the money you pay for a loaf of bread is divided among those who produce it. For purposes of this demonstration, this rubber ball — (Sis *bounces ball to Louie*) — thank you ... will represent a commodity on the open market. And this rubber ball — (Sis *throws again*) — thank you ... will represent another commodity on the open market. And this — (Sis *throws bread roll which doesn't bounce, of course*) — it's hard to get good help nowadays, this — (Sis *pitches bread roll into his hand*) — bread roll will represent one more commodity on the open market. Let's call this a loaf of bread. Now this ... (*juggles three objects into play*) ... is the open market. (*A quick run through a few juggling techniques*) Not bad for a Ukrainian, eh? Now in the production of a loaf of bread there are four areas. (*Starts to juggle again*) First of all we have Retail — packaging, distribution, and sales — profit and cost. (*Bounces ball off forearm; Sis gives a crash of tiny cymbals*) — thank you. Milling and Baking, profit and cost — (*bounces ball off thigh; cymbals*) — thank you. Other ingredients, and if you've had a slice of bread lately you'll realize that that is mostly chemicals — (*ball off forehead, cymbals*) — thank you. And finally we have the profit and cost of the farmer. Give me a drum roll please. (Sis *at a loss for a moment, the rubs cymbals; ball caught in the back of the neck*) Three years in the Ukrainian National Circus for that one. (*Resumes juggling*) You know that the average price of a loaf of bread right now at the supermarket is about seventy-five cents. This is divided among the producers in the following way: Retail ... (*juggles two balls in one hand while taking bite out of roll*) ... gets thirty-four cents ... (*juggles three objects*) ... Milling and Baking ... (*another bite*) ... twenty-four cents ... (*chewing, mouth very full; stops juggling*) ... water please ... (Sis *brings flask, he drinks; it tastes good, maybe not water*) ... a little more ... (*another swig; juggles again*) ... other ingredients ... seven cents ... (*another bite*) ... This leaves the farmer with ten cents. (*Small piece left*) But unfortunately, the price of production of, for example, wheat, is 8.1 cents. This leaves the farmer for all his hard work ... (*nibble*) ... one ... (*nibble*) ... point ... (*nibble*) ... nine ... (*nibble*) ... cents. (*Just a crumb left, which he juggles with two balls. Kicks crumb to audience. Family surrounds him with congratulations*)

The old folks

FIDDLER: I've been a farmer myself and just sold out a few years ago. Right now I play the fiddle. I'd like to play you one of my own compositions: "My Own Little Two-step". (*As he plays, the company comes in one at a time, and as they set chairs in a straight line facing the audience assume the characters of oldtimers. The fiddle tune ends when they are all in place*)

MR. GILLANDERS: When we got our money out of the co-op, it amounted to almost $5,000; so we decided to take a world trip. I had a teacher once who said a man should either write a book or take a trip around the world before he dies.

MRS. GILLANDERS: And you've done both now, haven't you?

MR. GIL.: Yes. Yes, I have. Anyway, we started off and we spent one day in Hawaii, a day in India, ...

MRS. GIL.: ... a day in the Philippines ...

MR. GIL.: ... a day in Egypt ... I could have spent longer in Egypt; it was interesting there. ...

MRS. GIL.: Yes, two days would have been nice.

(*Pause*)

MR. WILLIAMS: Oh, things were really different back then in those days than they are now. Whenever you went anywhere, if you were going to town or taking a little trip, you always left your door

"The Oldtimers Today" in the Guy Sprung Production of *Paper Wheat*. From left: Sharon Bakker, Michael Fahey, David Francis, Skai Leja, Lubomir Mykytiuk and Bill Prokopchuk. *The Melfort Journal*.

Sharon Bakker and Michael Fahey as the oldtimers.

unlocked. Anybody passing through and needing a meal or a place to stay, they just came in and helped themselves to what was there. And they'd leave a note telling you who they were and where they were going.

MRS.
WILLIAMS: And thanking you. Yeah, things are a lot different now.

MR. WILL.: They were a lot different then.

We used to have some fine dances in those days.

MRS. WILL.: Oh, yes!

MR. WILL.: We charged ten cents at the door and that was only if you had it.

MRS. WILL.: That would take care of the lights and fuel for the stove. And the ladies would bring the lunch for afterwards. You know the cakes and cookies and sandwiches, coffee and tea, and sometimes . . . something special . . .

MR. WILL.: We never had any alcohol at those dances, eh?

MRS. WILL.: Oh, no!

MR. WILL.: If you got thirsty you just had a drink of water.

MRS. WILL.: Yes. (*Nudges him. Whispers to him. Persuades him with her foot*)

MR. WILL.: I used to play fiddle at those dances for forty years.

MRS. WILL.: He played fiddle for forty years at those dances. And people came from miles around. Everybody'd be up there dancing away; and Bill would be up there fiddling away; and I'd be sitting there. Well, occasionally a gentleman

74

would come over and ask me to dance . . . but I didn't dance too much. Yes, we had some fine times back then. But it wasn't all like that. We had to work hard too. My dad homesteaded outside Regina, you know. And there was eight of us kids and we all had our chores to do. But my dad, my dad really worked to get that farm going and keep it going. When he passed away a few years ago, the estate came up, you know. And our son had a chance to take over his land. So did a cousin of his who is also a grandson. I told our son to let the cousin have it because then it would stay in the family name. He had my dad's name, you see. Besides, our son was already farming our land then. So he did that; he let the cousin have it. And you know, I cried when I heard that that cousin had sold my dad's land to anybody at all, just sold it to anybody at all.

SOD-BUSTER: I have seen the prairie roll out ahead of me without a fence, without a furrow, without a road or a house, straight through to the Missouri Breaks. And the gray-green grass dotted with silver sagebrush and flowering weeds just going on forever. Oh, it was a sight. I have fought prairie fires day and night. I have known what it is to be lost in a blizzard when home and family are far away. I have watched the wild lands become boxed and squared — tamed; tamed by the world's want for food, I guess. I was among the first men to break this soil for cultivation. I

David Francis and Skai Leja as oldtimers.

threshed the bumper crop of 1915 and I knew the desolation of '37. I've seen the coming of the railroad, radio, telephone, television . . . the cars, trucks, tractors, airplanes. And I was a part of the first co-operative in this country. Now I've lived to see my son worth a million and a quarter dollars. I don't know how that happened, I've always been a socialist. You know, I'd give it all to be young again. To hold my hands on the handles of a plough. To smell the warm earth and see it fall aside in waves, right to each side, smooth as water. I'd give it all to be young again and feel that I could change the world.

THE END

Musical Score

Roll Out

Roll out those rails. Roll out. Well,

Lou- is Ri-el —— he was on the rise with the

In- dians and the Me- tis and a bat- tle cry. We sent

troops on the rail- road to beat 'em at Ba- toche. Now

ship the im- mi- grants to pay the cost. I said Roll

out. Roll out. Roll out those rails.

Roll out those rails. Roll out.

The Prairie Wind

prai —— rie. And each of these winds has its time —— and the wind is-n't al- ways con- tra —— ry to- night it is blow- ing just fine. Yes the prai- rie wind is blow- ing soft- ly to- night. The winds fresh and hope- ful and clear———. Oh prai- rie wind keep on blow- ing just right. And blow me a boun- ti- ful year.

2. I'll wel-come the sweet smel-ling wind that brings rain
And the moist smell of earth giv-ing life to the grain
The fresh breez-es rip-pling the ten-der green wheat
And cool-ling the sweat up-on my back in the sum-mer
   heat.

4. I've known Au-gust winds that came cold and fast
And ham-mered the hail on an an-vil of brass
It rat-tled the win-dows and flat-tened my wheat
In less than an hour I was bat-tered and beat.

Homesick Blues

I wish I were in Liv-er-pool town where
I was born there are no trees no hum-ming bees nor
fields of wav-ing corn.
If you should pass my home — my most be-lov-èd
home — —
So fare thee well sweet Done — gal the Ross- es
and Gwee-dore. — I'm cross-ing the main o —
cean where storm-y bil-lows roll — .

(Sung a capella)

2. Choven chitayetsya sered vodi
Plesche o chvili veslo
Misyats siyaye biliyuts sadi
Z daleka viduo selo

3. Any traditional Latvian song (sung a capella)

84

Bessie Song

(Fiddle tag to be played as introduction and between chorus and verse)

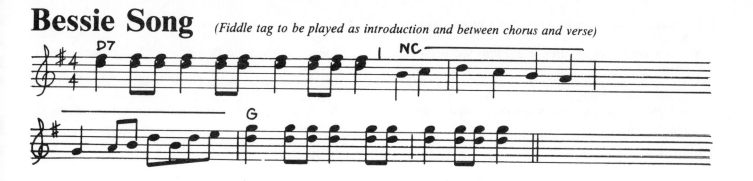

I drove a Mas-sey Fer-gus-son. I've run with the old John Deere,

But no-thing ev-er did the job like the Bes-sie I hold dear.

She can pull a plow or milk a cow, wash laun-dry on the board,

bend her back at the old wood-pile un-til she's cut a cord.

(CHORUS) "Oh Bes-sie, ——— some day you'll be hea-ven bound.

You'll go to meet you mak-er you'll be six feet un-der-ground.

But Bes-sie, ——— un-til the day that you're set free,

Get up ol' girl and do your chores, you're work-in' free for me.

2. I've seen her haul a rack of hay that'd break a camel's
   back,
   She bore me fifteen children in our little sod house
   shack,
   She's hauled our grain in the dead of night, pulled the
   horses from the mire,
   One night she nursed me through the flu and fought a
   prairie fire.

(CHORUS)

3. You can talk about your tractors 'til you're blue in the
   face,
   I wouldn't trade old Bessie for a hundred horse power
   Case.
   Oh, I seen better lookers with their hair all piled in
   tiers,
   But Bessie, she's a worker; we've been married fifty
   years.

(CHORUS)

Toiling

Toil-ing in the broil-ing sun boys, toil-ing in the broil-ing

sun we work all day ———— and we pray it'll last 'til the har-vest's

done oh Lord one time we ask for rain and the

next time we ask for sun it's a con-stant bat-tle and a

con-stant gamble and I think it's nev-er done

(REPEAT CHORUS)

The Grain Exchange Rag

long un-der-wear? We hold the cards; we know the tricks; You'll

ne-ver get us, 'cause we work in cliques

SPEAKING

It's free en-ter-prise, A--mer-i-can dream We'll

sell you down the ri-ver, but we'll ne-ver lose steam.

That's the Grain Ex-change, that's the Grain Ex-change, that's

SPEAKING

That's the Grain Ex-change Raaa-ag

The Man From Sintaluta

There was a man from Sin-ta-lu-ta, He had a vi-sion with-in his heart. He took the stand for the com-mon peo-ple A-gainst the power that was tear-ing them a-part. He said: "What are you wor-ried for? The worst they can do is kill you and if you be-lieve in Hea-ven; well, there is nothing to worry a-bout at all." Try to look from a-no-ther point of view; Let's all try to give and take. If we work to-ge-ther we'll a-chieve much more. So now is the time for us to co-op-er-ate Co-op-era-tive Com-mon-wealth,

Peo- ple work- ing for their own sur- vi ——— val.

We don't own the land, we on- ly farm ——— it. Pro-

duc- tion for use not pro- fit for the

few ———. "What are you wor- ried for? The

worst they can do is kill you, And if you be- lieve in

Hea- ven, well; There is nothing to worry a- bout at

all, ——— There is nothing to worry a- bout at

all ———."

Wheat Pool Song

Since the time of Jo- seph back in E- gypt ————. Right on down to

to- day Some- one else has ta- ken all the cream of the farm, and

left us the milk and whey. With a lit- tle real co- op- er- a- tion ————

We can help each o- ther a- long. Then all o- ver the land on

ev- er- y hand, we will shout and sing this song. From the

North, South, East, West all o'er the pra- irie keep the Wheat Pool rol- ling a-

long. Tell ev- ery- bo- dy when you sign your name.

Then ask your neigh- bor and he'll do the same. If we

all stick to- geth er what we have we'll hold. You'll be

proud to be a farm- er when the sto- ry's told. From the North, South, East, West

All o'er the prai- rie keep the Wheat Pool rol- ling a- long.

2. Farmer Jones made twenty thousand dollars
   speculating in wheat.
   Then the market dropped and he lost all that he had,
   And he came home badly beat.
   Had to buy some seed but had no money.

His neighbor said don't ever fear.
I'll divide up with you; I've enough for two
From my Wheat Pool cheque this year.

(CHORUS)

Co-op Song

Co-op-er-a-tion, what's it all a-bout?

There ain't no rea-son to jump and shout.

I want some mon-ey and a hot rod car. For-

get the North-ern lights and the prai-rie stars, I want to

get on the high-way and feel the wheels move,

Sell this land and get in the groove.

(CHORUS)

Co-op-er-a-tion shoo-bee-do-ah, Co-op-er-a-tion

shoo-bee-do-ah, Co-op-er-a-tion, shoo-bee-do-ah

Co-op-er-a-tion shoo-bee-do-ah, Co-op-er-a-tion

Co-op-er-a-tion, Just ain't part of my op-er-a-tion

Sas-kat-che-wan is real-ly get-ting to me

Take me big ci-ty I wan-na be free

93

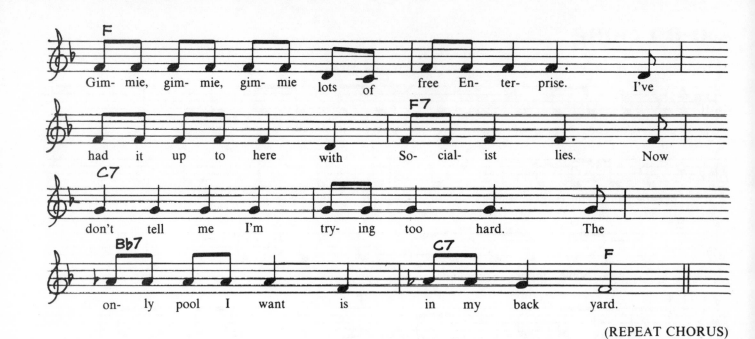

Gim- mie, gim- mie, gim- mie lots of free En- ter- prise. I've
had it up to here with So- cial- ist lies. Now
don't tell me I'm try- ing too hard. The
on- ly pool I want is in my back yard.

(REPEAT CHORUS)

Tour Itinerary

Tour Itinerary

FIRST TOUR — Spring
1977
Eston
Sintaluta
Moose Jaw
Regina
Saskatoon

SECOND TOUR — Fall
1977 — Provincial (including
five day appearance in
Toronto)
Saskatoon
Toronto
Prince Albert
Nipawin
Melfort
Humboldt
Wynyard
Outlook
Davidson
Moose Jaw
Assiniboia
Cabri
Shaunavon
Leader
Unity
Kerrobert
Rosetown
North Battleford
Lloydminster
Meadow Lake
Strasbourg
Weyburn
Melville
Canora
Moosomin
Yorkton
Raymore
Sintaluta

Radville
Spiritwood
Regina
Swift Current
Central Butte

THIRD TOUR — National,
Summer and Fall 1979
Calgary, Alberta
Vauxhall, Alberta
Hanna, Alberta
Medicine Hat, Alberta
Drumheller, Alberta
Pincher Creek, Alberta
Cardston, Alberta
Brooks, Alberta
Claresholm, Alberta
Edmonton, Alberta
Gibbons, Alberta
Stony Plain, Alberta
Wetaskiwin, Alberta
Grande Prairie, Alberta
Fairview, Alberta
Westlock, Alberta
Jasper, Alberta
Wainwright, Alberta
Vermilion, Alberta
Athabasca, Alberta
Meadow Lake, Saskatchewan
Maidstone, Saskatchewan
Prince Albert, Saskatchewan
Watrous, Saskatchewan
Preeceville, Saskatchewan
Grenfell, Saskatchewan
Estevan, Saskatchewan
Fox Valley, Saskatchewan
Kindersley, Saskatchewan
Gravelbourg, Saskatchewan
Moose Jaw, Saskatchewan
Regina, Saskatchewan

Saskatoon, Saskatchewan
Ottawa, Ontario
Vancouver, British Columbia
Guelph, Ontario
London, Ontario
Petrolia, Ontario
Hamilton, Ontario
Kingston, Ontario
Lennoxville, Quebec
Blyth, Ontario
St. Catharines, Ontario
Montreal, Quebec
Waterloo, Ontario
Toronto, Ontario